BEATING A RAP?

BEATING A RAP?
Defendants Found
Incompetent to
Stand Trial

Henry J. Steadman

THE UNIVERSITY OF CHICAGO PRESS
Chicago and London

HENRY J. STEADMAN is director of the Special Projects Research Unit, New York State Department of Mental Hygiene. He is the author of *Careers of the Criminally Insane.*

The University of Chicago Press, Chicago 60637
The University of Chicago Press, Ltd., London

© *1979 by The University of Chicago*
All rights reserved. Published 1979
Printed in the United States of America

83 82 81 80 79   10 9 8 7 6 5 4 3 2 1

Library of Congress Cataloging in Publication Data

Steadman, Henry J.
   Beating a rap?

   (Studies in crime and justice)
   Bibliography: p.
   Includes index.
   1. Criminal justice, Administration of—New York
(State)   2. Insane, Criminal and Dangerous—New York
(State)   3. Insanity—Jurisprudence—New York (State)
I. Title.   II. Series.
HV8145.N7S73   345'.747'04   78-21110
ISBN 0-266-77140-7

To Buford Rhea, Jr.

Contents

Tables and Figures

Preface

As with many areas, the institutions at the interface of the mental health and criminal justice systems are characterized more by sensationalism than by hard fact. What becomes the subject of the Sunday supplement or the national television networks' special report is usually the particularly bizarre, gruesome, or mishandled case, rather than the typical one. Too often such presentations do not probe the total picture. It was to produce such a total picture that this book was written.

When the research reported here was planned, its goals were at the same time modest and grandiose. The modest portion is what is reported here. We intended to select a sizable group of criminal defendants who were found incompetent to stand trial and follow them for three years to see what happened in mental hospitals, courts, and the community. Although straightforward, such research had never been done. Prior to this project, there was much conventional wisdom in law reviews and the media about the fate of incompetent defendants. The wisdom offered by the legal analysts highlighted lifelong commitment, while the media focused on defendants quickly escaping from lax mental hospitals to again pillage, rape, and murder. However, no one had taken a group of defendants who were sent for mental health treatment and determined what actually was happening under the statutes that had changed so dramatically throughout the 1970s. This was the modest research goal reflected in this book.

Some of the more ambitious goals of the research project related to assessing psychiatric predictions of dangerousness which were made for one segment of the group we followed. The results of these assessments and our subsequent application of statistical prediction techniques to the defendants' behavior are found in a range of other publications. The somewhat grandiose goals that our innate scientific optimism held out at the project's outset were attenuated as the research progressed. Regardless, these forays into predictions of human behavior are tangential to the core issues dealt with here. They are mentioned to alert the reader to the fact that only one portion of the project, which was funded for four years by a grant from the National Institute of Mental Health's Center for Studies of Crime and Delinquency (MH 20367), is reported here.

During the four years of federal support and the two more years of state-supported work, many people were crucial to the research. A person to whom the project is indebted for the encouragement to seek the funding in the first place is Dr. Elaine Cumming. She was aware of the pending statutory changes that presented the research opportunities and, as always, was perceptive enough to see their potential.

In the planning and implementation phases of the research, a number of clinicians who administered the facilities in which the data were collected were tremendously cooperative. Dr. John Wright opened the doors and educated us about forensic psychiatry. Drs. Erdogan Tekben, Stanley Portnow, Daniel Schwartz, and Paul Agnew all welcomed data collection in their facilities and offered many insights which greatly increased our understanding of the systems we were studying.

The four years of data collection depended upon many capable staff members. Two who worked particularly long and effectively were Terry O'Bryan and Gregg Bell. In addition, Jeraldine Braff, Jeremy Singer, Lydia Minatoya, Sara Lee, and Gwenn Turner all made substantial contributions in a wide variety of ways.

During the writing of the manuscript itself, a number of people provided special help. Nancy Burton did reanalysis after reanalysis, cleaning and running the data as well as critiquing the various drafts of the manuscript. Her commitment to the internal consistency in the data and to accuracy within the multitudinous subgroups was absolutely crucial. Joseph Cocozza, as he often has, provided a range of substantive comments on the early versions of the manuscript. Also, Gail Bullis, the one point of continuity through the entire research process, was especially conscientious in typing the manuscript.

No list of acknowledgments would be complete without mentioning the three people who make all my endeavors worthwhile—Carolyn, Sharon, and Jacquelyn, my three ladies. Without their interest and support in many ways, there would be insufficient incentive to push forward from the low points that are part of the research and writing enterprises.

Finally, the continuing commitment of the New York State Department of Mental Hygiene to quality scientific research was the *sine qua non* of this study. Surely the infusion of federal funds was important, but the contributions in staff time and the whole range of indirect contributions from the state of New York were essential. This fiscal and psychic support was, and is, provided without impugning the professional autonomy of the individual investigators beyond that appropriate for the protection of the clients who are research subjects. Just as many stereotypes about the incompetent defendant are broken by the data reported here, so too are many false images that the scholarly community holds of agency research shattered by the milieu for research that typifies the Special Projects Research Unit.

1 Incompetency Diversion: The Best of all Worlds?

Periodically, brutal or bizarre acts of murder or assault bring into the public eye psychiatrists working in the criminal justice system. In the mid 1970s, the Patty Hearst case highlighted the psychiatrist's role in the courtroom in relation to the issue of competency to stand trial. After Ms. Hearst was captured and charged with bank robbery and assault with a deadly weapon, her defense attorney had her examined by a number of psychiatrists to show that she was not mentally able to stand trial. The state mustered psychiatrists who said she was competent to stand trial. After listening to this battle of experts, the court concluded that she was able to stand trial. More recently, with as much notoriety, the New York City case involving David Berkowitz, "The Son of Sam," brought the issues of competency to stand trial again into public view, with the same result as in the Hearst case. One psychiatrist said Berkowitz was incompetent to proceed with his trial, while the state hired other psychiatrists who said he was competent. Again, the court agreed with the latter experts; Berkowitz was indicted and he pleaded guilty to murder, for which he received a 25-years-to-life sentence.

One of the controversies that is addressed nearly every time such cases reach national proportions is the idea that incompetency is a ploy used by defense attorneys to enable their clients to escape from criminal charges. The question is whether the defendant is just "beating a rap." Major difficulties in assessing whether or how often defendants "beat a rap" include confusion over exactly what the criminal and psychiatric issues are in competency hearings and what the results of the procedure are.

The "Son of Sam" case mentioned above illustrates what goes on. David Berkowitz was arrested in August, 1977, as a suspect in the murder of six New York City women and the wounding of seven other victims with a .44-caliber handgun. Immediately after arrest and arraignment, Berkowitz was remanded for psychiatric evaluation to the psychiatric prison ward of Kings County Hospital in Brooklyn. The questions posed to the examining psychiatrists by the police and the court had little to do with either the bizarre notes found in Berkowitz's apartment or his mental state at the time of the alleged shootings. Rather, the court asked for a medical opinion about whether Berkowitz had the capacity to proceed with his trial. To be fit to proceed, he was required to have the mental capacities to fully comprehend the charges against him, to understand the court proceedings that would result from the criminal charges, and to be able to cooperate with an attorney in his own defense.

If Berkowitz had been found incompetent to stand trial, he would have been committed under New York's Criminal Procedure Law for one year to a maximum security mental hospital run by the Department of Mental Hygiene. During this year he would have received psychoactive drugs, group psychotherapy, individual psychotherapy, or some combination of these treatments. The treatments would have been aimed at restoring his mental capacities to the point where he could meet the threefold standard for proceeding with a trial. This does not mean that he would necessarily be free from all forms of diagnosable mental illness found in the Diagnostic and Statistical Manual of the American Psychiatric Association. Rather, it means that no remaining symptomatology existed sufficient to interfere with his thought processes and thus prevent him from proceeding to trial.

If competency were regained at any time during the first year's commitment, Berkowitz would have been returned to Brooklyn for the continuance of his trial as part of the regular routine of the New York City Supreme Court. If he did not regain competency during this first year, his case would have been reviewed by the Kings County court that committed him at the end of his first commitment order. He could be recommitted if the judge remained convinced that he was still unfit to proceed to trial. This periodic renewal of commitment orders would continue in New York for a maximum of two-thirds of the maximum sentence for the crime with which the individual is charged. When this maximum is reached, criminal charges are terminated. If continued psychiatric treatment is deemed necessary, a request for commitment under the mental health codes has to be initiated. However, in the case of murder, where the maximum sentence is life, maximum retention would be the point when fitness to proceed is never expected to be reached. At that time, under the U.S. Supreme Court's *Jackson* v. *Indiana* decision, civil proceedings are required for retention under the mental health codes.

In Berkowitz's case, all these contingencies were avoided when, on October 22, 1977, and again on April 24, 1978, the state supreme court in Brooklyn found him fit to proceed. The questions that received the brunt of media attention in his case were those dealing with whether Berkowitz was criminally responsible for his actions at the time of the alleged murders, whether he was not guilty by reason of insanity, and his transfer in July, 1978, from Clinton Correctional Facility to Central New York Psychiatric Center. The questions of mental state at the time of the murders and after sentencing, while intriguing, are irrelevant for our purposes. We are concerned with what happens to individuals, who, unlike "Son of Sam," are found incompetent to stand trial before their trials and are sent to state mental hospitals. These persons are picked up by the police, initially processed in the usual way by the police and the courts, and then diverted from the criminal justice system into the mental health system. This type of diversion may either delay or terminate the criminal proceedings, depending upon the specific state's statutes and the length of the hospitalization.

Incompetency diversion in the criminal justice system is thought by the eminent forensic psychiatrist Dr. Alan Stone to be the "...most significant mental health inquiry pursued in the system of criminal law. Its significance derives from the numbers of persons to whom it is applied, the many points in the criminal trial at which it can be applied, the ease of its being invoked, and the consequences of its application" (1975:200). The best estimate of the number of people diverted as incompetent each year in the United States is around 9,000. This group represents about one-quarter of the approximately 36,000 for whom the issue is raised. The question of competency is raised most often shortly after arrest, but may be introduced at any point in the criminal process right up until the sentence is imposed. Thus, persons are occasionally found incompetent to be sentenced *after* they have been convicted. The issue of incompetency is relatively easy to raise. Just about any party involved in the arrest, prosecution, defense, or arraignment may request psychiatric examination of the defendant.

The consequences of being found incompetent to stand trial are debatable. There is some documentation, notably in the work of the former director of legal medicine in Massachusetts, Dr. A. Louis McGarry (1973), that those persons found incompetent spend substantially more time involuntarily detained in maximum security hospitals for the criminally insane than they would have spent in prison had they been convicted of the crimes with which they were charged and incarcerated. On the other hand, many people believe that diversion of actual or alleged criminals into mental hospitals allows them to "beat a rap."

The public seems suspicious of all types of criminal justice diversion programs, of which incompetency is but one. Any program that allows a person arrested for a crime to avoid prosecution and return directly to the community is viewed with great concern by the public. Such suspicions, and fears, have been common problems as all types of criminal justice diversion programs have expanded in the community treatment movements of the 1970s (Scull 1977). Despite public concern, diversion remains a popular concept in criminal justice program planning. As Elizabeth and James Vorenberg observe, "no word has had quite the power of 'diversion' which offers the promise of the best of all worlds: cost saving, rehabilitation and more humane treatment" (1973:152).

Diversion promises fewer cases will have to be heard in the courts, thus saving taxpayer dollars by decreasing the costs of pretrial detention. Furthermore, allowing arrested persons to avoid criminal convictions and prison terms diminishes their subsequent criminal careers through community-based rehabilitation, rather than encouraging a lifetime of crime through extensive contacts with other, possibly more skillful, criminals in prison. Thus, through diversion, the state supposedly saves money, the arrested person is treated more humanely, and the risk of subsequent crimes is reduced. Everyone is better off because of diversion.

Unfortunately, the realities of criminal justice diversion are neither as clear-cut nor as positive as they may appear at first glance. First, diversion encompasses many different things. It may mean incompetency, on the one hand, or the directing of landlord-tenant disputes, neighborhood fights, and family arguments to special noncriminal hearings presided over by law students on the other.[1] Most often, it refers to formal programs involving rehabilitation professionals that take a person after arrest and, before the court passes judgment or accepts a guilty plea, sidetrack him to some type of program intended to decrease the chance that the same criminal behavior will occur again.[2] This intervention may be a weekend outpatient program for alcoholics, involuntary commitment to a state mental hospital, or a lecture.

The most salient characteristic of any type of diversion is that individuals who could have been or were arrested are put back into the community on the promise that the prescribed treatment will be a more effective deterrent than prison. As has been often observed, these programs merely formalize the daily discretion required of the police officer, who arrests but a small portion of those people who could be detained.

Some striking examples of the public view of incompetency as diversion were apparent in reader comments solicited by the Albany, New York, *Times-Union* after a series of incidents happened in the Albany metropolitan area involving persons who at one time had been found incompetent to stand trial and were eventually returned to the community. In response to the newspaper's request for his opinion, one rural resident replied, "We have too many sob sisters who think more of insane criminals than of good-living citizens." Another resident in the same July 14, 1974, issue commented, "I don't think society is adequately protected because of the number of crimes committed by people that have been confined to institutions. I think the whole system must be changed..."

Similar views were expressed by Patrick Violante, whose son

was shot in the eye when "Son of Sam" shot Tracy Moscowitz, his last victim. After the court hearing in which the first psychiatrist's report found Berkowitz incompetent to stand trial, Violante said to an NBC-TV reporter: "I think he's as sane as anybody else. I think it's just a cop-out, and I don't think he's going to get away with it. I have a lot of faith in the law, and I still will and I always will have, but if he's able to get away with this type of tactics this changes my idea..."

The types of situations most community members seem to be referring to are described by Alan Stone as occurring when, "...in the lower criminal courts the judge is often willing to accept outpatient treatment, day care, even once-a-week group therapy as an alternative for criminal sanctions which carry a high penalty. Whatever stigma the [mental illness] label may carry, many defendants gladly accept it rather than a prison sentence" (Stone 1975). This situation, however, is not similar to that of incompetent defendants. More often, their situation is that found in a survey of records in the Detroit, Michigan, Recorder's Court. This survey of 21 incompetent defendants committed to Ionia State Hospital concluded that the hospital "...is often used as a place to incarcerate persons without benefit of trial. When this period of incarceration is ended the state apparently considers that adequate punishment has been accomplished. Thus it appears that the emphasis in fact is not on the protection of the accused but on the protection of society" (Hess et al. 1961).

Despite such findings, and other characterizations of incompetency hospitalization as the "poorest and most restrictive form of hospitalization" (Foote 1960), the public's perception remains one of criminals easily and quickly returning to the street through the conduits of state mental hospitals. What makes it so difficult to support or refute these fears is the paucity of data available on incompetent defendants after they have been found unfit to proceed with their trials. Who are these people? How did they get to the point where they were found incompetent? Did they have long prior police or mental hospitalization records? Have they been troublemakers in their communities for years? What happens to such defendants after they are found incompetent to stand trial? Do they return to the streets quickly, or after long stays in mental hospitals? If some return to the community quickly and others after lengthy stays, are there significant differences in the amount of trouble these groups cause after their respective returns?

Although most of these questions are basic, there is almost no information with which to answer them. Some useful data are available on certain aspects of some of these questions, but there has been no study of a large group of these defendants from the point of their determinations of incompetency by the courts until they return to the community and are again at risk of arrest. It is from such a study that this book grew. This study takes all 539 males charged with felonies who were found incompetent to stand trial in New York State between September 1, 1971, and August 31, 1972, and examines who they were and how they were found incompetent to stand trial. It then follows them through the mental hospitals to which they were sent, to the courts to which some were returned for continuance of their criminal processing, and finally back to the street to see how they lived upon returning to the community and what trouble, if any, they got into back on the street.

We will see that those persons found incompetent to stand trial are a diverse group. They range from 16 to 72 years of age, although most are young. The group's average age is 31. They are predominantly nonwhite. Slightly over half of these defendants never married. Their education varies from almost no formal education to completion of college. Most complete either the ninth or tenth grades in high school. Most defendants have prior police records (73% have prior arrests). They average nearly three arrests and almost two convictions each. The vast majority of these offenses are not juvenile adjudications, but reflect adult offenses. There is a considerable difference in what types of prior crimes these defendants were involved in, just as there is a considerable difference between those indicted for the offense which led to their incompetency determination and those who were not indicted at the time they were found unfit to proceed. Of those who were indicted, about 55 percent had prior arrests for murder, assault, manslaughter, or rape, whereas just under 40 percent of the indicted had records for such violent crimes.

A history of prior mental hospitalizations along with a prior police record greatly increases a defendant's chance of being found incompetent. Fully 80 percent of the 539 males in our study group had previously been hospitalized. The average length of prior mental hospitalizations was almost two years. Thus, while the picture of these defendants demonstrates the great diversity that exists within this often narrowly stereotyped group, it is also evident that a substantial number of defendants found incompetent to stand trial have fairly lengthy prior arrest records and mental hospitalizations.

Because the group of incompetent defendants diverted from the criminal justice system we studied were charged with felonies, the crimes with which they were charged are quite severe, not only compared to all arrests in New York during the same time period, but also when compared with all felony arrests. For example, while 0.8 percent of all felony arrests statewide were for murder, 15 percent of the incompetent defendants were so charged. Reciprocally, 21 percent of all felony arrests in New York were for drug-related offenses, while only 3 percent of the incompetent defendants were charged with drug offenses. Thus, based on the prior criminal record of these defendants and on the charges they are facing, there is considerable support for the public's apprehensions that they are "getting off" from some very serious charges by means of mental health diversion.

Whether one views the mental health diversion experiences of the defendants we studied as "beating a rap" probably depends on three factors: (1) how long they remain hospitalized; (2) the environment of the hospitals to which they are committed; and (3) the outcome of their criminal charges after their hospitalizations. The third question must be answered by comparing these defendants with a group of defendants from the same jurisdictions who are not diverted. We will see that the length of time spent in maximum security hospitals varied widely and that there were major differences between those defendants indicted and those not indicted prior to the determination of incompetency. These differences were primarily related to the greater seriousness of crimes for those who were indicted.

More important than the amount of time that was spent in mental hospitals for the questions about whether incompetency diversion is an easy way out are the conditions of hospitalization. The picture of civil mental hospitals, where patients have considerable freedom of movement and from which escape is quite easy, is inappropriate for the locations at which these defendants were detained. Rather, the settings are prisonlike, with locked wards, security officers, and barbed-wired fences. The picture that remains after spending many days in these maximum security hospitals is that they are not desirable places to live. There is a substantial level of patient-patient assault; homosexuality, both

consenting and nonconsensual, is common; and guards are sometimes unnecessarily brutal to patients. In sum, for many patients this is a much less desirable place to do time than prisons,
where they know the ropes.

The final question was about total time served. To determine
this, it is necessary to add together all mental hospitalization time,
time awaiting trial before and after the incompetency determination, and any time that results from a subsequent conviction after
return to stand trial. This total detention time can then be compared with that of defendants processed entirely within the usual
mechanisms of the criminal justice system. Among the group of
incompetent defendants we followed, there was very little difference in the total amounts of time served between those diverted
and those not diverted. The incompetent defendants were convicted more often than a comparable group of nondiverted defendants, but the sentences the incompetent defendants received
were more often time served or probation. Thus, the time spent in
mental hospitals becoming competent to stand trial was apparently counted as incarceration time by the judges.

Putting these factors together, there appears little to distinguish the experiences of defendants found incompetent from
those defendants who are never diverted from criminal justice
procedures. It is simply doing time in a different setting. Some
persons prefer that setting; others do not. The picture presented
by the incompetent defendants after they return to the community is similar to that presented by a strictly ex-convict group.
Overall, then, we will see that there is much less difference
between incompetent defendants and the vast majority of other
criminal defendants who are not involved in any criminal justice
diversion programs, whether or not mental health services may be
part of such diversions.

To develop this picture of who the incompetent defendant is,
where he came from, why he is found incompetent, what happens
to him in mental hospitals, prison, and the community this book
will follow him from the point he is found unable to proceed with
his trial because of mental illness. Chapter 2 presents some
background on the procedures used to collect the data and to
follow the defendants. Chapter 3 describes in detail the defendants who were followed. Chapters 4, 5, and 6 focus on the
various stages of the defendants' criminal and mental health
processing, including the competency hearing at which the psy-

chiatric testimony was accepted by the court, their maximum security detention, their opinions and perceptions of this detention, and their experiences when returned to stand trial. Whether the experiences of this large group of incompetent defendants suggest that they have in one way or another "beaten" the criminal justice system through their diversion will be examined in chapter 7. Chapter 7 also considers what the experiences of these defendants suggest about the incompetency plea itself and the rights of society to protect itself. The epilogue looks at how these persons fared when they did return to the community. It is based on crime data and some interviews with selected defendants and their families.

As the picture of the incompetent defendants are fleshed out from these data, it is useful to keep in mind that this is one type of diversion from the criminal justice system which may lead either to termination or to delay of the criminal disposition. What types of dispositions ultimately occur, under what types of circumstances, and with what frequency are not well known. However, they are important because they relate to many of the current controversies in the rehabilitation versus punishment goals of incarceration. In the incompetency plea, no one may proceed toward a conviction unless the defendant is mentally equipped. If he is not, he is provided with indefinite, involuntary psychiatric treatment and medication. This humane ideology may lead to rapid return to the street, where subsequent violence may occur. In contrast, it may lead to mental hospitalization much in excess of the probable criminal sanctions that would have been imposed. A third alternative is a fairly rapid return to the community—at major savings of correctional and mental health costs—of a person who will not engage in further criminal activity and who will be better able to function in environments hostile to human habitation. Just how often each of these scenarios is actually played out is the focus of this book. Is the fate of the defendant found incompetent to stand trial such that he effectively "beats the rap?" If so, how often does this occur and at what cost to society? First, we turn to how our data were collected and what we knew about incompetent defendants before the information on these 539 people was available.

2   The Starting Points of the Study

The research on which this book is based was undertaken for two reasons. First, the available information about persons found incompetent to stand trial and about what happened to them after this determination was totally inadequate to develop rational policies for their care and detention. Second, despite the absence of information, a substantial revision of New York's Criminal Procedure Law in 1971 radically altered how incompetent defendants were treated. This revision provided an unusual opportunity to address a set of important questions. The first reason may seem surprising, given the abundance of articles in legal and psychiatric journals on the uses and abuses of incompetency. However, these articles concentrate on the legal principles involved, the roles appropriate for the psychiatrist in the legal process, how to distinguish between incompetency and insanity, and the insanity defense. Only rarely are there any facts about the incompetent defendants themselves.

The second reason relates simply to opportunity. Like most states in the early 1970s, New York vested most of the responsibility for the detention and treatment of incompetent defendants with the state agency responsible for the maintenance of the prisons, the Department of Correctional Services (DSC). After a person was found incompetent to stand trial, he or she was sent to a DCS maximum security hospital for the criminally insane. The New York facility was Matteawan State Hospital. Traditionally, defendants sent to Matteawan were inincarcerated for exceedingly long periods and received minimal treatment at best. The conditions of deprivation at Matteawan and at New York's other hospital for the criminally insane, Dannemora, were noted in a 1969 United States Court of Appeals case involving an inmate at Dannemora, *Schuster* v. *Herold* (410 F.2d 1071 [1969]). Circuit court judge Irving R. Kaufman wrote:

By its very nature, confinement at an institution for the criminally insane is far more restrictive than at a prison. Nothing more dramatically illustrates this difference than the petty indignities to which inmates in the former are subjected. For example, their visiting and correspondence rights are curtailed. In the appendix we reproduce a *pro se* petition by a prisoner in a similar institution in Massachusetts listing at least thirty-five such differences illustrating that these seemingly small but numerous indignities may accumulate to the point where the prisoner-patients consider them the most galling of all restraints.

In an attempt to remedy some of the defects apparent under the correctional model for the treatment of incompetent defendants, the 1970 New York legislature, as part of its overhaul of the state's Criminal Procedure Law (CPL), revamped the procedures for detaining incompetent defendants. The revision attempted to return defendants to trial more quickly after they were found incompetent. This was viewed both as more humane and cheaper because many of the incompetent defendants' criminal charges were sufficiently minor that little or no incarceration would result from them. Thus, responsibility for the incompetent defendants was taken away from the Department of Correctional Services and given to the Department of Mental Hygiene (DMH). The assumption was that civil mental hospitals would be more effective in rapidly returning defendants to stand trial than the DCS facilities had been. The CPL required that all incompetent defendants be treated within DMH facilities, with one exception. Those incompetent defendants who were charged with felonies and were indicted would also be evaluated as to their dangerousness. Only those defendants who were determined not to be dangerous would go to DMH hospitals. The dangerous defendants would continue to be detained in Matteawan under DCS auspices.

One feature of the legal landscape that was an extremely important influence on the implementation of the CPL and on the progress of our research was a July, 1972, decision of the United States Supreme Court, *Jackson* v. *Indiana* (92 S.Ct.854 [1972]). After *Jackson* there were legal guidelines limiting the detention of the incompetent defendants. None had existed previously. The decision gets its name from Theon Jackson, a deaf, retarded mute who was arrested in Indiana for two robberies amounting to nine dollars. Because of his communication deficits and mental impairment, he was found incompetent to stand trial. He could neither understand the charges against him nor adequately cooperate with his attorney in building his defense. After being found incompetent, Jackson appealed. He claimed that this determination was the equivalent of a life sentence without being convicted because it was improbable that any of the factors causing his incompetency would respond to psychiatric treatment. After his petition for a new trial was rejected by both the local trial court and the Indiana Supreme Court, the U.S. Supreme Court reversed the lower courts and said Jackson could not be committed for an indefinite period as incompetent.

The effect of this decision was to establish for the first time guidelines to prevent the long-term, and in many cases lifetime, commitment of unconvicted persons under criminal statutes. Henceforth, they had to be released from incompetency commitments when there was a reasonable probability that within the forseeable future competency would not be regained. Thus, the experiences of the 539 defendants in this study occurred within current legal guidelines.

New York is fairly typical of the United States in both its statutes and facilities for treating and detaining incompetent defendants. It is atypical only in that in 1971 it had two maximum security correctional hospitals for the criminally insane. Most states only have one such facility. Therefore, most of what is said about the experiences of the incompetent defendants selected for study from New York applies to most other U.S. jurisdictions.

THE COMPLEXITIES OF INCOMPETENCY PROCESSING

One difficulty in examining what happens to a large group of incompetent defendants in correctional and mental hygiene institutions results from the complexities of the processes. Some of these complexities are demonstrated by the well-known "Son of Sam" case mentioned in chapter 1. David Berkowitz was arrested on August 12, 1977; booked at a precinct police station for murder; and arraigned the following day in Brooklyn, the location of his last alleged murder and assault. During his arraignment, a defense attorney suggested that he be transferred to the psychiatric prison ward of Kings County Hospital for psychiatric tests to determine his ability to proceed with a trial. The State Supreme Court judge agreed to this examination and signed a 30-day commitment order for evaluation.

Two and a half weeks later the psychiatric report was delivered to the presiding judge. This report indicated that "...despite the presence of a rather elaborate paranoid delusional system, the question of this defendant's fitness to proceed is not that simple. He is well aware of the charges against him, understands that by society's standards his acts were criminal and has the intellectual capacity to learn whatever there is about the legal proceedings that he does not already know. The problem is that his psychosis prevents him from assisting in his own defense. In the first place he feels he [is] so emotionally dead that the outcome of his case is totally immaterial to him" (*New York Times*, Sept. 2, 1977, p. 5).

After the contents of this report were made known, the Brooklyn district attorney requested permission for an independent evaluation of Berkowitz's fitness. The court approved this request. At the competency hearing on October 20 and 21, 1977, the court had to decide between the initial psychiatric report finding Berkowitz incompetent and the second finding him competent. Ultimately it ruled that Berkowitz was in fact competent to proceed with his trial.

While the Berkowitz case illustrates some aspects of competency proceedings, it is also misleading. The Berkowitz legal and psychiatric maneuverings clearly indicate that the most common course of incompetency events is arrest and arraignment, followed fairly closely by the question of incompetency, most often raised by the defense attorney. When this question is raised, the defendant is sent to a special psychiatric ward for evaluation. This evaluation phase, in fact, has wide variability. In less densely populated areas, psychiatrists are more apt to come to the county jail for the examination. Upon completion of an examination, a report is submitted to the court where the criminal charges are pending. If the defendant is found incompetent by the psychiatrists, a hearing ensues, during which the judge decides to accept or reject the medical opinion. There is some variation between jurisdictions on whether a hearing is required. In New York a hearing occurs only if there is medical opinion that the defendant is unfit to proceed. In other jurisdictions, once an examination has been mandated by the court, a hearing may be required, regardless of the psychiatric findings.

Just what information psychiatrists should offer the court is much debated (GAP 1974). It may even be persuasively argued that psychiatric opinions on competency have little place in the process at all. Incompetency is a legal question, and it should be up to a lawyer to decide whether he or she can work with a given defendant to develop an appropriate defense. Also, there is a question whether psychiatrists' reports should provide conclusory statements about competency or whether their reports should be limited to symptoms, diagnosis, and prognosis, leaving the decision as to how these effect competency to the judge (GAP 1974). The most common procedure is exemplified by the excerpt from the initial psychiatric report on David Berkowitz cited above. The examining psychiatrists gave not only symptoms and diagnosis, but also their opinions about competency. Based on these facts and opinions, plus defense and prosecution cross-examination of the psychiatrists and the defendant, the judge reached a decision.

Another of the major problems in dealing with incompetency is the confusion of lawyers, psychiatrists, and judges, who mix incompetency with insanity and the not-guilty-by-reason-of-insanity (NGRI) defense. Competency issues pertain to the defendant's mental state at the time of trial and sentencing, while the insanity defense relates to mental state at the time of the commission of the alleged act. It makes little difference to the determination of competency to stand trial how impaired someone was when the alleged crime occurred. For incompetency, some mental disease or defect must interfere sufficiently with the defendant's ability to comprehend the charges against him, to understand the judicial process in which he or she is involved, or to cooperate with an attorney in his or her own defense. It is quite possible to be mentally ill and be competent to stand trial. However, this possibility is usually not recognized or accepted by judges. Furthermore, a significant proportion of psychiatric reports submitted on competency actually deal with insanity at the time of the alleged offense. Sometimes this results from a request by the court to examine a defendant on both issues at the same time. More often, however, it is a result of psychiatrists providing the court with inappropriate testimony.

In fact, a major issue in whether being found incompetent is "beating a rap" is the association between being found unfit to proceed with trial and a subsequent disposition of not guilty by reason of insanity when the criminal trial finally occurs. One widely held view is that many or most defendants found incompetent eventually are found NGRI, thus beating the system. Actually no data document this. It remains an open question, despite public and professional views to the contrary.

As was noted above, much of what happened in the Berkowitz case was atypical of incompetency proceedings. First, the majority of cases that involve questions of competency are not murder cases, let alone multiple murder cases. In the group we studied, murder cases made up only 14 percent of all cases. Second, there are few cases in which either the defense or prosecution obtains an independent examination in addition to that provided by the court-appointed psychiatrists. While there may be two psychiatrists involved in the original examination for the state, it is unusual to obtain a second independent examination. Such a second opinion may be most frequent in murder and multiple murder cases. In such instances, the district attorney is apt to have more evidence than usual, which increases the probability of conviction. As a result, he is anxious to proceed with the criminal trial. In lesser offenses there is usually more difficulty in developing a case. Therefore, diversion into a secure facility via incompetency detention allows retention until the case can be prepared for more effective prosecution or until the hospitalization time spent regaining competency is long enough to serve in lieu of prison time. Thus, a difficult or insignificant case is removed from the district attorney's files.

The final atypical feature was the amount of publicity the Berkowitz case received. Most cases involving incompetency involve less serious offenses committed by marginal individuals completely uninteresting to the public. Some indications of the effects of skewed press coverage in these matters was evident in a small study done in conjunction with the large-scale project described in this book. In that study (Steadman and Cocozza 1978), every person cited as being criminally insane by a random sample of the general public was charged with or convicted of murder, kidnapping, or bombing. This despite the finding mentioned earlier that murder makes up only 14 percent of all the charges against incompetent defendants. The respondents mentioned such notorious figures as Patty Hearst, "Squeaky" Fromm, and Charles Manson as being criminally insane. All of the persons mentioned had the question of incompetency raised during their highly publicized trials, but none was actually determined to be incompetent.

Although these features of the Berkowitz case may be out of the ordinary, the proceedings of the case are useful in setting the groundwork for understanding the circumstances of incompetency diversion. How little was actually known at the beginning of this research about the characteristics and processing of incompetent defendants is apparent in the next section of this chapter.

WHAT DO WE KNOW ABOUT THE INCOMPETENT DEFENDANT?

Demographic Characteristics
There is an astonishing lack of information about who the people are who are found incompetent to stand trial. It would seem logical to have a fairly comprehensive picture of these defendants, given the many analyses of problems associated with incompetency procedures, but this is not the case. Authors dealing with the uses and abuses of the incompetency process rarely provide any description of the people found incompetent. Two recent examples are the highly regarded overview of mental health law by Alan Stone (1975) and the Group for the Advancement of Psychiatry's (GAP) 1974 report. In Stone's chapter on "Incompetency to Stand Trial," a variety of issues, such as how the competency process works and how it ought to work, are covered, but there is not a single piece of information about the characteristics of the defendants found incompetent. Similarly, the oft-quoted sixty-page GAP report highlights many key issues surrounding incompetency and offers a number of controversial recommendations, yet it provides no information about the characteristics of the incompetent defendant.

While it may not be too unusual for psychiatric or legal

treatises to omit specific data on the defendants themselves, it is most surprising to see the same thing occur in the research reports. A prominent example is a seminal article by two psychiatrists (Hess and Thomas 1963) that reported their analysis of the functioning of the incompetency statutes in Michigan and the practices associated with these statutes in Ionia State Hospital. This landmark analysis cogently analyzed the misuse of incompetency and the confusion of the concepts of insanity and incompetency. The authors sampled 1,484 patients in Ionia State Hospital to obtain four study groups totaling 119 subjects. There is much discussion about the hospital and court records used as data sources. However, nowhere in this important article is a single piece of information given about the characteristics of the incompetent defendants in Ionia or in the study groups, except that there were wide variations in age and psychiatric diagnosis.

Needed information about who incompetent defendants are is also missing in two studies of the evaluation procedures for incompetency determinations. Studies by Pfeiffer and colleagues (1967) and Lacko et al. (1970) both offer considerable information about their respective study groups of 85 and 453 subjects who were sent to clinics for psychiatric evaluation of competency. However, neither study gives any indication of the characteristics of those defendants who were found incompetent. In the Pfeiffer study, where 91 percent of the defendants sent for competency evaluation were white, the reader can infer that the majority of those who are actually determined to be incompetent will also be white. Beyond such inferences, these two studies give no information about the incompetent defendant.

The most recent study of defendants diverted for competency evaluations by Cooke and colleagues (1974) displays the same problem. They report that the average age of the 205 defendants referred for competency evaluation was about 31, the majority were unmarried, their mean education was some high school, and about 54 percent were white. Again, however, no information is provided about how the characteristics of the defendants who were actually found incompetent by the Michigan courts may vary from all those defendants diverted for evaluation.

McGarry and Bendt (1969) stated that courts "tended to commit the very old and the very young, alcoholic, and the non-psychotic in a civil status. Men in their middle years with large numbers of previous misdemeanor arrests—classified perhaps as public nuisances—tended to be hospitalized in a criminal status" (p. 96). Other than this general statement, though, there was simply no information available to tell us about the people who are actually found to be incompetent to stand trial.

Only recently, during our project's data analysis, has a report been published that provides needed information on the characteristics of the incompetent defendant. This report, by the National Clearinghouse for Criminal Justice Planning and Architecture (Roesch and Golding 1977), is an evaluation of the procedures and facilities employed in North Carolina for determining competency. The authors drew a sample of persons released between 1971 and 1975 from the state's maximum security hospital after regaining competency. Of the 130 defendants they studied, 94 percent were male; 53 percent were white; only 25 percent were currently married; their mean age was 36 (apparently at the time of discharge, although this is unclear from the report); and their mean educational attainment was approximately the seventh grade. These characteristics suggest that blacks, unmarrieds, and males were highly overrepresented among incompetent defendants in North Carolina, compared to the state's population as a whole.

Length of Stay

The theme struck by Hess and Thomas in their 1963 report on Michigan incompetency procedures that "the result of Michigan's management of the problem of incompetency is the incarceration, often for life, of persons without benefit of trial or the safeguards of civil commitment procedures" (p. 716) has received continuous support in the research on incompetency right up through a similar statement by the Group for the Advancement of Psychiatry's 1974 report. GAP concluded, "These principles underlying the requirement of competency give heavy emphasis to protection of the defendant. It is therefore ironic, . . . that the finding of incompetency may well result in the worst possible outcome for the defendant—a lifetime sentence to a hospital for the criminally insane."

The data used to support such conclusions come both from case studies and larger surveys. Hess and Thomas, for example, discuss a sixty-year-old man in Ionia State Hospital who was committed as incompetent in 1926 on charges of gross indecency. In the early 1960s, he was still there under the diagnosis of "simple psychosis." Some further data from Illinois (Tuteur 1969) showed that eight patients who were provided special psychiatric assistance in regaining competency after long-term hospitalizations had been hospitalized for from two to eleven years in special security hospitals. In the McGarry and Bendt pilot study of conditions in Massachusetts discussed above, the six males who were criminally committed had an average length of hospitalization of four and a-half years on relatively minor charges.

The most comprehensive and incriminating evidence available about excessively long confinements for incompetent defendants is that offered by McGarry's large-scale study. In a four-year study of incompetency practices in Massachusetts, McGarry and his coworkers selected 219 incompetent defendants who were being detained in Bridgewater State Hospital in 1963. Each of these 219 defendants was given special psychiatric reevaluation to determine his or her current state of competency, using a series of newly developed assessment instruments. The average length of special security hospitalization for the 56 defendants who were returned to trial upon review was 4.3 years. For the remaining 163, the average hospitalization was 14.9 years.

While these data from three states, and the conclusions drawn from them by the GAP report, suggested unequivocal consensus on the issue of excessive hospitalization of the incompetent defendant, such closure may be premature. All of the research studies that report on extremely long detentions in special security hospitals for these defendants refer to research subjects who happened to be in a hospital after being found incompetent. None of these studies followed a group of defendants found incompetent and assessed how long they were hospitalized. The one study that did a retrospective longitudinal examination of these questions was done in New York. Vann (1965) took records from Erie County, where Buffalo is located, for a group of twenty-seven males charged with felonies and found incompetent to stand trial. Court and district attorney's records permitted a determination of how long they had been hospitalized before returning for trial or having their charges dropped for thirteen of these twenty-seven defendants. Four of the thirteen had been returned to trial. These four were hospitalized for an average of 9 months, ranging from 3 months to 20 months. The person hospitalized for 20 months was charged with manslaughter; the other three were charged with grand larceny. In another four of the thirteen cases, indictments were dismissed while the persons were hospitalized. The average length of hospitalization for these four was 29 months, with a range from 13 months to 52 months. The person hospitalized 52 months was charged with arson, as was one other defendant. Two were charged with assault and extortion. Five defendants remained in the special security hospital. For these five, the average length of hospitalization was 74 months, with a range from 12 months to 120 months.

These data about the length of hospitalization for incompetent defendants demonstrate that a wide variation exists. Much of this variation appears to be related to the seriousness of charges. Those hospitalized in the last group were charged with such offenses as murder, assault, and carnal abuse of a child. Most of these incompetent felony defendants charged with less severe property offenses were returned to court shortly after admission. Thus, the frequently cited conclusion that a determination of incompetency is akin to a life sentence is not strongly supported by the available data. These data suggest, rather, that there is tremendous variation in length of hospitalization. Furthermore, the research from which these data are taken is so inadequate as to render any conclusions premature.

A second major question about the validity of the GAP report's conclusion relates to the possible impacts of the *Jackson* decision discussed above, which occurred after the research under discussion was done. Supposedly, *Jackson* would preclude the indefinite confinement of the person cited by Hess and Thomas who had been hospitalized since 1962 on a charge of indecent exposure. *Jackson* requires that if there is not a reasonable probability of a person's regaining competency within the foreseeable future, the defendant cannot be detained in a mental hospital except by resorting to the civil mental health statutes for involuntary commitment. Thus, not only are there questions about the empirical underpinnings for some of the conclusions of lifelong hospitalizations associated with incompetency determinations, but there is even more question about what has happened since the 1972 *Jackson* decision. If the decision has had the intended impact, there should have been a noticeable decline in the length of pretrial incompetency diversions. Our follow-up on 539 incompetent defendants, then, is not only the first comprehensive analysis of a cohort of such defendants, but also offers the initial large-scale assessment of systems of incompetency post-*Jackson*.

Inappropriateness of Detention
One finding of prior research about the detention of incompetent defendants that cannot be called into question is the demonstration of the inappropriate detention of many defendants. In 1966, the National Institute of Mental Health provided a grant to A. Louis McGarry, then director of legal medicine in Massachusetts, to support the project previously referred to. One goal of this project was to develop reliable and valid instruments for assessing incompetency to stand trial. Two hundred nineteen residents of Bridgewater State Hospital who had been found incompetent to stand trial had their current levels of competency evaluated. Of the 219, 56 (25.6%) were found ready to stand trial, despite their being retained as incompetent by the Bridgewater psychiatric staff. Furthermore, of the 219 patients selected for study, another 15 (6.8%) were returned as competent after they were known to be part of the study population. Thus, 33.4 percent of the persons being detained as unfit to proceed with their trials were actually capable of being returned to court. However, without the impetus of these special evaluations, most would have remained at Bridgewater.

Additional support for the frequency of inappropriate detention in special security hospitals comes from Illinois. Thirty-six patients were transferred from Illinois Security Hospital to Elgin State Hospital and became part of special research and treatment efforts (Tuteur 1969). Of the 36, 8 were returned as competent within one to twelve months after transfer. During the first year, another 3 were released directly to the community because their charges were dropped. So 11 of the 36 patients (30.5%) transferred and given special attention were returned to competency within a year.

While only these two projects have provided and reported on this special type of evaluation and treatment, the consistency of their experiences gives preliminary indication that as many as one-third of the persons held in special security hospitals as incompetent may be capable of standing trial.

Final Disposition of Criminal Charges

One of the crucial questions about whether the incompetent defendant is "beating a rap" is what happens to him when he regains competency. Four previous studies looked at the issues of how many were convicted and what sentences they received. These studies show few consistencies. McGarry's work in Massachusetts found that 71 defendants were returned to stand trial after an average of 4.3 years of hospitalization. Of these, 33 (46%) were convicted, 24 (34%) were not prosecuted, and 14 (20%) were found to have been not guilty by reason of insanity. Of the 33 convicted, 14 received prison sentences. A Detroit study (Matthews 1970) examined the final dispositions of 21 alleged homicide offenders between 1959 and 1963. After "long" periods of hospitalization, 18 (86%) had their charges dismissed, 2 were found guilty of manslaughter, and only 1 (5%) was found not guilty by reason of insanity.

Two other studies were done in New York. Vann's data from Erie County, discussed earlier, suggest that those patients who were returned to stand trial within a year tended to be convicted. A larger group of patients who served longer times in Matteawan had their indictments dismissed while hospitalized. The largest group, with the most serious offenses, such as murder, assault, and robbery, remained hospitalized for an average of nearly six years. Apparently the more serious the offense, the longer the hospitalization, and the lower the conviction rate.

The second New York State study, done on a larger scale than Vann's, examined statewide outcomes. The New York City Bar Association examined all 235 cases returned to trial from Matteawan in 1964. In sharp contrast to the Erie County data, where 58 percent of the cases had charges dismissed, only 9 percent of the 235 cases statewide had their charges dismissed after an average of four years of hospitalization in maximum security confinement. Two-thirds of the cases resulted in a guilty plea, most often to a reduced charge where the sentence was "time served," that is, no additional imprisonment was ordered by the court, which accepted the time done in Matteawan as sufficient for the conviction charge.

The one point of consistency among these four studies appears to be Vann's observations that ". . . in the majority of cases the court has allowed the confinement to a criminal mental hospital to serve as compensation to society for a prison sentence" (p. 31).

Thus, where a defendant spends four or five years awaiting trial, conviction rarely results in further incarceration. When the defendant regains competency within a year, the conviction rate is higher, and he or she is much more apt to receive additional prison time, even when the offense is less serious than that of the defendant who spends more pretrial time hospitalized. Those defendants with the most serious charges appear to be punished less because their ultimate conviction rates are relatively low, compared with what would have happened within the criminal justice system. However, their total times incarcerated may not be vastly dissimilar.

The earlier studies were inconclusive about what percentage of the defendants, especially those with murder charges, are finally found to be not guilty by reason of insanity and are sent to low security civil mental hospitals. McGarry found 20 percent of his group was ultimately NGRI, whereas in the Detroit homicide study, only one of eighteen was found NGRI. Unfortunately, none of the existing studies can directly answer the question of whether these dispositions and pretrial hospitalizations result in "beating a rap" because they do not calculate the total time spent in detention and compare these figures to those among the criminal population who were not diverted. Because this study has the statewide data on all 539 defendants found incompetent in New York over a one-year period, it will be able to address these questions more fully.

At the beginning of our research, we knew next to nothing about the characteristics of incompetent defendants. We knew somewhat more about their experiences after they were found incompetent. For the most part, there is substantial variation in how long they remain in maximum security mental hospitals. For many, this hospitalization extends far beyond the point where they could be returned to stand trial. What happens after return to trial is the least clear, except that quite often hospitalization appears to be seen as a substitute to prison. Overall, we know much more about certain phases of the processing of the incompetent defendant than we know about the persons themselves. It remains to be determined whether or how often this criminal justice diversion does result in "beating a rap."

NEW GROUND
The available research studies lacked the proper methodology as

well as the needed information. Until now, no one has taken a large group of incompetent defendants from the point that they are determined to be incompetent by the court and followed their progress through the mental health and criminal justice institutions. By so doing, and by describing these defendants, data become available to answer the numerous questions about the actual results of such diversion more adequately. It is precisely such a longitudinal study of a large cohort of incompetent defendants that we present.

The diagram in figure 1 facilitates understanding the experiences of these defendants. The first event in the sequence is arrest. This may be followed by the question of competency being raised, as happened to the "Son of Sam," or it may be followed by arraignment on the charge and detention in jail to await trial. The initial psychiatric evaluation may occur within a few days after arrest, or it may take place after many months of imprisonment while awaiting trial. In either case, those defendants who were part of the group we followed had all been arrested, evaluated by psychiatrists, and found by the psychiatrists to be unfit to proceed with their trials. Our follow-up included all male defendants the court found incompetent in a one-year period throughout New York State. It included no one referred for evaluation who was found competent. Based on the estimates we obtained from the psychiatrists doing these evaluations and on prior research studies, we determined that about 25 percent of those referred for evaluation are found incompetent. Therefore, we will make few generalizations about the arrest and evaluation process portions of the incompetent defendants' experiences. However, the information obtained on these defendants did permit analysis of their backgrounds prior to this incompetency determination.

After being found unfit to proceed with their trials, the defendants under study went to maximum security hospitals. For the most part, they remained in these hospitals until they regained competency or until charges against them were dropped. If competency was regained while charges were pending, they were returned to stand trial. Where the charges were dropped, the persons were usually transferred to regular security state mental hospitals until they met medical standards for release or they absconded. Most of those defendants against whom charges were dropped while they were hospitalized eventually returned to the community, along with many of those who returned to stand trial.

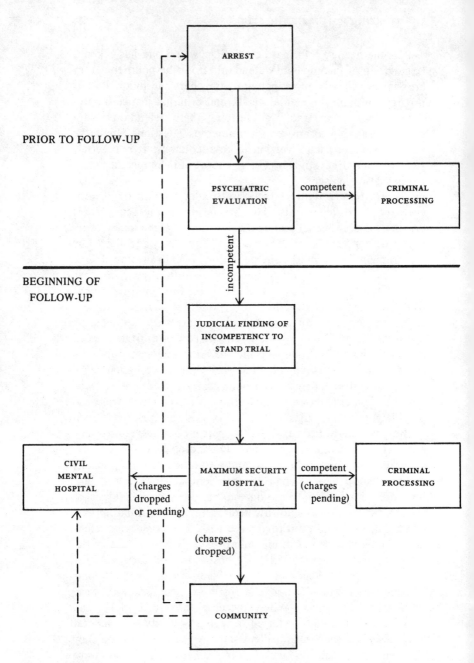

Fig. 1 Schematic Outline of the Institutional Processing of the Study Group

The latter group sometimes returned immediately to the community after being found not guilty or after being found guilty and given a sentence of "time served," with their hospitalization time considered as sufficient for the conviction.

We will take all 539 males charged with felonies who were found incompetent to stand trial between September 1, 1971, and August 31, 1972, and examine what happened to them for the next three years. We concentrate first on who they are. Having looked at their characteristics and at their criminal and mental hospital histories, we will follow them through the mental health and criminal justice systems to answer the question Did they "beat a rap?" To answer this, we will examine their experiences in the maximum security mental hospitals to which they were sent and in the criminal courts to which some of them returned. Does being found incompetent amount to a lifelong sentence without the protections of due process in the criminal or civil processes? Or does it, as the public perceives it, more often amount to "beating a rap?"

3   A Profile of the
        Incompetent Defendant

The first goal of the research was to determine exactly who the people were who were found incompetent to stand trial. Between September 1, 1971, and August 31, 1972, in New York, 539 males who were charged with felonies were found incompetent to stand trial by the courts. This chapter profiles, in detail, these 539 defendants in four areas: their demographic characteristics, their prior mental hospitalization histories, their prior criminal histories, and the crimes with which the defendants were charged when found incompetent. The information on their criminal records and their current charges is particularly important in assessing whether their diversion into mental health facilities amounts to "beating a rap" because many of the charges facing them when incompetent were for such violent crimes as murder, robbery, and assault.

DEMOGRAPHIC CHARACTERISTICS

Table 1 shows the group of 539 defendants as young, predominantly nonwhite persons with few community roots. The average age of the group is 28. However, there is a wide age range among the 539 defendants. The youngest incompetent defendant was 16; the oldest was 72. Ten percent of the defendants were over

45. The heterogeneity of the group is also evident in their racial characteristics: 46 percent black, 20 percent Hispanic, 2 percent Oriental and American Indian, and 33 percent white.

The average age of the incompetent group is approximately that of all males in New York State in 1970 (29), but it is somewhat older than the median age of all males arrested in New York in 1975, which was 24. Compared to all male inmates in New York prisons in 1975, there are somewhat more whites among the incompetent defendants. As of December 31, 1975, 56 percent of the New York prison census was black, 16 percent Hispanic, 27 percent white, and 0.4 percent other.[1] Overall, the racial distributions of the incompetent defendants and the state's prison population are quite similar.

TABLE 1   Characteristics and Mental Hospitalization Records of Study Group

Median age at incompetency		28
Race:	Black	45.6%
	White	32.8%
	Hispanic	19.9%
	Other	1.7%
Marital status:	Never married	54.6%
	Divorced, separated, widowed	28.6%
	Currently married	16.8%
Median grade attained		9th
Highest occupation held:	Executive, manager	9.4%
	Clerical/sales	11.1%
	Skilled manual	12.6%
	Semi-skilled	17.7%
	Unskilled	37.2%
	Never employed	11.9%
Regularity of employment:	Regular	15.3%
	Irregular	35.0%
	Rarely, if ever	49.7%
History of drug abuse:	Some	41.8%
	None	58.2%
History of alcohol abuse:	Some	38.5%
	None	61.5%
% with previous mental hospitalizations		81.5
Average number of months hospitalized		29

As is the case for most offender populations, there are a number of other differences between the demographic characteristics of these defendants and statewide population figures. For example, the median year of school completed for all males statewide is twelfth grade; for the incompetent defendants, it was only ninth grade. There are also substantial differences in marital status between the state population as a whole and these incompetent defendants. Only 17 percent of all 539 incompetent defendants were married, but fully 65 percent of males statewide are married. As would be expected from the significantly below average educational achievements of these defendants, most of those who have worked have been employed in unskilled jobs and have had irregular employment histories. Thirty-seven percent of these defendants never exceeded unskilled jobs such as janitor, car wash employee, dishwasher, and the like. Another 10 percent were never employed. However, it is important to note that, while the defendants rate below population distributions, as with age and education, they are a mixed group. In fact, 9 percent had at some time held upper-level executive and management positions, and 11 percent had worked in responsible clerical and sales positions.

Where there is substantially less diversity among the incompetent defendants' occupational experiences is in the regularity of their employment. Only 15 percent were considered to have worked regularly, that is, to have been employed at least six months in the year prior to their most recent arrest. Another 35 percent worked irregularly. This latter group would be defined as unemployed by government figures, since they appeared to take work when they could find it. The remaining 50 percent were neither working nor looking for a job. In fact, 54 of the 539 defendants had never worked.

Overall, the demographic picture of these incompetent defendants is one of marginal individuals with much less than average education and few useful job skills. Most have few community ties, either through employment or family. An unusually high proportion have never married. They appear to be a marginal group, many of whom have been and continue to be shuttled back and forth between mental hospitals and prisons.

From table 1 it is evident that the study group has had much difficulty with drug and alcohol abuse and has had prior contacts with mental hospitals before the current findings of incompetency. Of the 539 defendants, 225 (48%) had a record of heavy drug use. Eighty-five percent of these were using drugs in the six months prior to their current arrest. To a lesser extent, there was a history of alcohol abuse evident in the records of these defendants. Thirty-eight percent of the 539 had such a history. Most of those who had abused alcohol (86%) had done so within six months prior to their current arrest.

We were surprised to find what an extremely high proportion of the incompetent defendants had had prior mental hospitalizations. The prior research had given no indication of how common previous hospitalization was. Fully 81 percent of these defendants had at some time been in a mental hospital. Not only were most of these defendants previously hospitalized, but these hospitalizations were not short-term. The median length of time hospitalized for those who were admitted was 29 months, nearly two and one-half years. The average 29 months of hospitalization was accumulated over an average of four hospitalizations, for an average length of stay of 7 months. However, there is wide variation that should not be masked by these averages. Eighteen percent of the 539 defendants had no prior hospitalization, while 68 of the 539 (13%) had accumulated total hospitalization time of more than six years.

Some of the typical as well as the variable features of the lives of these defendants can be seen in the two case histories below. The first, David Thomas, is an "average" case.

David Thomas was 26 years old when found incompetent. He was born in Redbank, New Jersey. According to his clinical notes, he had a happy and normal childhood. He went as far as the ninth grade, then quit school to go to work. He never held a steady job, but worked for a time as a laundry worker, busboy, auto mechanic, and shipping clerk. He married at 18, but this relationship was stormy, with many arguments and fights. He was separated from his wife for some time prior to being found incompetent. He had been in and out of state mental hospitals over a dozen times in the two years preceding his incompetency determination. He had never been arrested prior to his arrest for reckless endangerment. The circumstances of this arrest are unclear from his records, but apparently he got into a heated argument with his wife and began fighting with her. The police were called and Thomas arrested. He was found incompetent to stand trial. On admission he was diagnosed as paranoid schizophrenic.

The disruptive life-style, limited job skills, irregular employ-

ment, and previous mental hospitalizations seen in David
Thomas's life were common among the 539 incompetent defendants as well. However, even in this socially marginal group,
there is great variation in education and employment.

Some of these variations are evident in the considerably different case of Jeffrey Steiner. Born in August, 1941, Steiner had
an unremarkable childhood. He obtained a masters degree in
education in 1969 and was employed for two years after that as a
teacher. He was married in late 1970. His wife had their first
child in November, 1971. Shortly after the birth of this child,
Steiner began working two jobs. He felt that his wife was neglect-
ing him. On December 27, 1972, using two milk containers full of
gasoline as fuel, he set his Queens apartment on fire, doing
substantial damage not only to his apartment, but also to the
four apartments above his. Steiner was arrested on December 28
and admitted to Long Island Jewish Medical Center the following
week. From there he was returned to court to be indicted on
arson, second degree, the charge pending when he was found
incompetent. Prior to this hospitalization he had received no
psychiatric treatment and he had no police record.

PRIOR CRIMINAL RECORDS

The defendants' criminal histories confirm the impression, first
intimated in the medical and mental hospitalization records of
these defendants, that prior to the current finding of incompetency many defendants have continually been shuttled back
and forth between the mental health and criminal justice facilities. We have divided the defendants into two groups, those who
were indicted at the time they were found incompetent to stand
trial, and those who were unindicted.[2] The data in table 2 indicate clearly why this division was introduced.

Both the indicted and the unindicted defendants have had
much contact with police and the courts throughout their lives.
However, those who became part of this study group after being
indicted had much longer and more severe histories than those
who were unindicted. While practically two-thirds of the unindicted had previously been arrested, 81 percent of the indicted
defendants had prior arrests. Not only were more of the indicted
defendants previously arrested, but they also had been arrested
and convicted more often.

TABLE 2   Prior Criminal Records of Study Group

	Unindicted (N = 282)	Indicted (N = 257)
Percent with prior arrests	66.3	80.5*
Average number of prior arrests	2.7	3.8*
Average number of prior convictions	1.3	2.2*
Percent with prior violent crime arrest	38.7	56.0*
Average LDS score	2.9	4.7*

* All differences significant at .001 based on *t* test.

If the severity of a criminal record is considered along with its length, it is evident that the indicted defendants differ from the unindicted defendants. Fully 56 percent of the indicted had previously been arrested for crimes of murder, manslaughter, assault, or rape. Thirty-nine percent of the unindicted had also previously been arrested on such charges. To obtain some overall indication of the seriousness of criminal records, we devised a scale that considered both length and severity of criminal records. This scale, called the Legal Dangerousness Scale (LDS) (Steadman and Cocozza 1974), ranges from zero, or least serious, to 15, or most serious. The indicted defendants averaged 4.7; the unindicted defendants averaged 2.9. The unindicted group was involved in many prior serious criminal activities, but the group's average was significantly less than the average of those defendants who had been indicted. In both groups, many defendants go back and forth constantly between hospitals and jails. For instance, 132 defendants (24%) had three or more prior arrests and three or more prior mental hospitalizations. It seems safe to conclude that these defendants are quite familiar with both the criminal justice and mental health systems.

CURRENT CRIMINAL CHARGES
As with prior criminal records, there are substantial differences between the indicted and the unindicted defendants on the offenses for which they were found incompetent. Furthermore, there are also some very significant differences between the charges facing these incompetent defendants as a whole and the charges on which persons were arrested throughout New York State.

Table 3 displays the charges facing the defendants under

study. The differences between the indicted and unindicted are readily apparent. One-quarter of the incompetent defendants who were indicted were charged with murder, but only 6 percent of those unindicted had murder charges. The same disparity is evident in robbery charges; another quarter of the indicted defendants were charged with robbery offenses, but only 15 percent of the unindicted were facing these charges. On the other hand, burglary and assault appear much more often among the unindicted than among the indicted defendants. It appears that when the charges are of the highest severity, such as murder and robbery, the district attorney is much more apt to obtain an indictment at a very early stage of the criminal processing. Where crime is less severe, the district attorney is less apt to seek an indictment. Upon a finding of incompetency to stand trial, the absence of an indictment may be even more significant, since it can represent an easy way out for the district attorney and the state. They get a person off the street for an indeterminate time in a maximum security facility without criminal prosecution. It remains to trace the careers of these incompetent defendants to assess how often incompetency may turn out to be an easy way to detain an individual without the additional trouble and expense of further criminal prosecution.

TABLE 3   Crimes with Which Study Group Was Charged When Found Incompetent (9/1/71–8/31/72)

Charge	Unindicted ($N = 282$)	Indicted ($N = 257$)
Murder	5.7	25.7
Manslaughter	.4	.8
Robbery	15.2	25.3
Assault	21.0	11.3
Burglary	24.8	15.6
Arson	8.2	5.8
Rape	2.5	3.9
Grand Larceny	6.0	3.5
Drug	2.1	3.1
All others	14.2	5.1

Regardless of these issues, it is quite clear that those persons found incompetent to stand trial in New York in the year from which this sample was drawn were charged with some serious offenses and that they had fairly lengthy and serious prior criminal records. Fully 15 percent of these defendants were charged with murder, 20 percent with robbery, and another 16 percent with assault.

The case of David Abel illustrates some of the more common group patterns of continuing criminal activity. Born in May, 1948, Abel was one of ten children. He started school at the age of five and quit in the tenth grade at age fifteen. Soon after quitting school he entered the armed forces and served for two years in Viet Nam, receiving an honorable medical discharge. After his return to civilian life, he had no record of working. Between 1964 and 1971, he spent about five years in prison for convictions on petty larceny, burglary, criminal trespass, and possession of a dangerous weapon. Just prior to his 1964 arrest for robbery, he spent two months involuntarily committed in a state mental hospital. He was released, although his condition was listed as "unimproved." In early 1971, Abel was released from prison and, according to the psychiatrists making the competency determination, began using LSD four or five times a week and taking amphetamines intravenously daily. In October, 1971, he was arrested for murder. This was reduced by the grand jury to manslaughter, unauthorized use of a motor vehicle, grand larceny, and criminal possession of stolen property. Records such as Abel's, with multiple prior arrests and a current charge involving physical violence to a person, were common among the 539 incompetent defendants, especially those indicted.

The severity of the charges faced by these incompetent defendants is particularly startling when these offenses are compared to those of all felony arrests in New York. The year closest to that in which the incompetent defendants were arrested was 1971. Table 4 displays the distribution of all of 1971's nearly 115,000 felony arrests. The tremendous differences between this distribution and that of the incompetent defendants is obvious.

Of the approximately 115,000 felony arrests in 1971 in New York, 0.8 percent were for murder. Among the 539 defendants found incompetent, 15.2 percent were charged with murder. Thus, murder is eighteen times more frequent among the incompetent defendants than among all those people arrested for felonies in New York. Likewise, arson is much more frequent among the incompetent defendants, occurring thirteen times more often than would be expected based on statewide felony arrest rates. To a lesser extent, robbery and assault are also more common among the incompetent defendants.

TABLE 4   Felony Arrest Charges in 1971 for Males in New York State and for Study Group (9/1/71–8/31/72)

Offense	1971 arrests*		Incompetent defendants		Incompetency determinations per 1,000 arrests
	N	%	N	%	
Murder	941	.8	82	15.2	87.1
Arson	525	.5	38	7.1	72.4
Rape	1,593	1.4	17	3.2	10.7
Manslaughter	363	.3	3	.5	8.3
Assault	12,012	10.4	88	16.3	7.3
Robbery	15,355	13.4	108	20.0	7.0
Burglary	21,346	18.6	110	20.4	5.2
Grand Larceny	12,347	10.7	26	4.8	2.1
Drug	23,803	20.7	14	2.6	.5
All others	26,658	23.2	53	9.8	2.0
TOTAL	114,943	100.0	539	100.0	

* "Adult Male Arrests for Felonies as Reported by 634 New York State Police Agencies," New York State Department of Correction, Division of Research, 1972.

On the other hand, drug-related offenses are the most frequent felony arrest charges statewide, making up 21 percent of all felony arrests in New York in 1971. Yet among the incompetent defendants, these offenses represent only 2.6 percent of all charges. Likewise, the property-related offenses of criminal possession of stolen property and forgery comprise 5.9 percent and 4.4 percent, respectively, of all felony arrests, but make up only 0.9 percent and 0.6 percent of the charges pending against the incompetent defendants. Overall, then, there is a consistent and strong tendency for the incompetent defendants to be charged with violent crimes against persons and to be charged less often with drug and property offenses than would be expected on the basis of all New York arrests.

These data on the current criminal charges of the incompetent defendants under study suggest that the "raps" to be beaten are, on the whole, quite serious. They are the types of offenses which justifiably concern the public. If persons arrested for murder, robbery, and arson are successfully beating the courts and police by getting diverted to mental hospitals from whence they rapidly return to the community, there is indeed cause for alarm. However, if mental hospitalization simply precedes normal criminal processing, where convictions and sentencing eventually occur, this diversion becomes much less threatening.

In sum, we are examining questions about the type and length of detention of incompetent defendants for a group facing serious criminal charges and a group who has been there before. They have spent substantial time in jails and mental hospitals. Their backgrounds strongly suggest that the incidents that got them into our study were part of a long-term career of illegal and incompetent social behavior that has often been associated with shuttling back and forth between the courts, jails, and mental hospitals. These people are marginal in every sense of the term. They have much below average education, they have limited job skills, and they have worked very irregularly when employed. They are predominantly nonwhite and are usually not married. They have few community roots. Based on their criminal histories, they might appropriately be seen as a very threatening group of individuals. If they do "beat their raps," there is cause for grave concern.

The first step in examining the questions surrounding the real impact of incompetency is to look at the judicial hearings which found the defendants incompetent.

4   The Competency Hearing

This chapter is the first of three successive chapters that follow the defendants' progress through the courts and mental health facilities. An incompetent defendant is initially sidetracked for psychiatric evaluation after the defense attorney, or the judge arraigning him on criminal charges, or someone else, raises the possibility that he is not competent to stand trial. However, incompetency is a judicial decision that is made at a hearing after psychiatric evaluation. Thus, the competency hearing is actually the fourth major event in the processing of incompetent defendants. Before the hearing, the defendant has been arrested, he has been officially charged by the court with the crimes (arraignment), someone has raised the question of whether he is fit to stand trial, and psychiatric evaluations have taken place. All this happens *before* the competency hearing.

The psychiatrists doing the competency examinations in New York City estimate that only one-half to one-quarter of those for whom the question of competency is raised receive, or should receive, psychiatric evaluations. Furthermore, of those who are evaluated, only about one-half are found incompetent. This means that the incompetent defendants described in chapter 3 represent only about 25 percent of all those defendants for whom the question of competency was originally raised.

In New York State a competency hearing is required only if the defendant is determined by the examining psychiatrists to be incompetent. If there is no psychiatric evidence of incompetency, the defendant simply is returned to jail to await trial. Unless some of the examining psychiatrists find the defendant unfit to proceed with a trial, the court cannot determine the defendant to be incompetent. Some defendants who have a competency hearing may be found by the courts to be fit to proceed with a trial, despite contrary psychiatric opinion. However, all defendants who are found incompetent have had competency hearings. Since it is the incompetent defendants who are the focus of this book, the competency hearing is a crucial aspect in understanding their movements through the courts.

THE PROCEDURES

Once a question of a defendant's competency is raised, the court must decide whether there is sufficient cause to warrant a psychiatric examination. If there is, the judge signs a thirty-day Order of Examination. This gives the state a month either to transfer the defendant to a site for psychiatric evaluation or to bring two psychiatrists into the jail to examine the defendant.

All the examinations of the defendants we studied were done by psychiatrists. In many jurisdictions, notably Tennessee (Laben et al. 1977), there is a strong trend toward having other mental health professionals, such as psychologists, psychiatric nurses, and social workers, do preliminary screening of defendants for whom questions of competency have been raised. In those states, only after initial screening suggested a high probability of incompetency would a psychiatrist be called upon to evaluate the defendant. Massachusetts tried psychiatric screening before pretrial commitment to a state hospital and found that the percentage of those found incompetent by psychiatrists rose dramatically because nearly half of the defendants whose competency was questioned were determined to be competent by the preliminary screening. The procedures in effect in New York during our study offered no such formal screening. Instead, for every defendant whose competency was questioned, two psychiatrists would examine the defendant within thirty days of the Order of Examination and submit a report in a standard format to the court. Figure 2 shows a copy of a blank report. This report was provided to the court in enough time to permit a hearing within the thirty days

EXAMINATION REPORT

(Psychiatric examination, C.P.L. Article 730)

STATE OF NEW YORK

_____ COURT

COUNTY OF _____

THE PEOPLE OF THE STATE OF NEW YORK VS _____ DEFENDANT	EXAMINATION REPORT Docket No. Indictment No. Information No. Charge _____ , _____ . in violation of § _____

    I, the undersigned, duly certified pursuant to law as a qualified psychiatrist or a certified

psychologist, having been designated by _____ ,

Director of _____ ,

pursuant to an order signed by Hon. _____ , (Judge) (Justice)

of the _____ court, _____ county,

dated _____ , to examine the above-named defendant, pursuant to

Article 730 of the Criminal Procedure Law, to determine if the defendant is an incapacitated defendant,

have conducted such examination with due care and diligence.

    The nature and extent of the examination was as follows: _____

_____

_____

    I have come to the following opinion as a result of such examination:

(NOTE TO EXAMINER: If the following paragraph sets forth the opinion of the examiner, sign the report where indicated below and do not complete Page 2. Otherwise, strike out the following paragraph, complete fully the remainder of this report and sign on Page 2.)

    It is my opinion that the above-named defendant does not as a result of mental disease or defect lack capacity to understand the proceedings against him or to assist in his defense.

SIGNATURE: _____ ,   DATED: _____ , 19 _____
    (Print name ·)   )
    (Qualified Psychiatrist)   (Certified Psychologist)
          STRIKE OUT ONE

FORM 704 DMH (10/71)   *(Continued)*

Page 2 - EXAMINATION REPORT (Psychiatric examination, C.P.L. Article 730)

It is my opinion that the above-named defendant is an incapacitated person in that the said defendant as a result of mental disease or defect lacks capacity to understand the proceeding against him or to assist in his own defense. My opinion is based on the following:

1. History and Clinical Summary, including Mental Status: *(Attach additional sheets, if necessary)*

2. Diagnosis:

3. Prognosis:

4. Reasons for my opinion, specifying those aspects of the proceedings wherein the defendant lacks capacity to understand or to assist in his own defense: *(Attach additional sheets, if necessary)*

(NOTE TO EXAMINER: If the order of examination has been issued by the Supreme Court or the County Court you must also complete the following, setting forth your opinion as to whether the defendant is, or is not, a dangerous incapacitated person.)

It is my further opinion that the above-named defendant (is) (is not) a dangerous incapacitated person, that is, an incapacitated person who is so mentally ill or mentally defective that his presence in an institution operated by the Department of Mental Hygiene is dangerous to the safety of other patients therein, the staff of the institution or the community. The following is a detailed statement of the reasons for finding the defendant to be a dangerous incapacitated person: *(NOTE: No statement is necessary if defendant is not so found)* allowed under the Order of Examination. Quite often the Orders were renewed. The actual length of time between arrest and the competency hearing in our group averaged eleven weeks. These psychiatrists' reports were presented to state supreme court judges because all defendants were charged with felonies, and in New York State all felony cases are heard in the state supreme court.

The supreme court judges read the reports while listening to testimony from the examining psychiatrists and to cross-examination from the defendant's legal representative and the district attorney. Based on this testimony and on the report, the judge determined whether the defendant was capable to stand trial or was incompetent and required treatment in a mental hospital. The period of commitment was set by law: for defendants not indicted, it was 90 days; and for those indicted, it was one year. These were the maximum commitments. If competency was attained in less time, the defendants could be returned to trial. If at the end of the initial commitment, competency was not regained, another hearing for continued detention was required. These renewal hearings could occur until the defendant had been detained as incompetent for two-thirds of the maximum sentence for the crimes with which he or she was charged.

The Dangerousness Issue

Before describing the hearing sites and the dynamics of the competency hearings, there is a side issue that should be mentioned. During the period when our competency hearing data were gathered, there was a second issue with which the courts were required to deal for those defendants who were indicted: whether or not they were dangerous. For our purposes, the dangerousness issue was peripheral. However, in many hearings we observed, it was a central procedural issue, since only those defendants found dangerous could be sent to the Correction Department's maximum security hospital. All incompetent defendants who were unindicted, and those indicted but not dangerous, had to be cared for in Department of Mental Hygiene facilities. As we will see in more detail in chapter 5, the determination of dangerousness made little difference. In the first six months of the study, the Correctional and Mental Hygiene treatment facilities were simply different wards within the same building and were staffed by the same correction officers and psychiatrists. Nevertheless, dangerousness issues did introduce some complications into these hearings beyond issues directly related to competency. In most jurisdictions, dangerousness issues do not relate to competency proceedings. Therefore, this issue will receive little further attention in this report.

How the Hearing Data Were Gathered

Competency hearings are closed hearings, where high security is maintained. Hearings occur in each of New York State's 61 counties. To observe enough hearings to draw any conclusions, we decided to observe at the two hearing locations in New York with the highest volume of cases in 1970. Both locations, Bellevue Hospital and Kings County Hospital, were in New York City, and both received referrals from the court and completed the psychiatric examination and the hearings within the facility by having the supreme court justices and the other court officers come in once a week. As best we could determine from the competency hearing reports submitted from the state's other 59 counties, the hearings we observed were typical, except that those in other counties were usually held at the county court rather than within the confines of the facility where the evaluations were done.

To determine what occurred at the competency hearings, we attended hearings for 26 weeks during the first year of the CPL. Over the 26 weeks that hearings were attended at Bellevue and Kings County, we observed 129 of the 539 hearings (24%) that involved defendants in our study group. After obtaining the necessary clearances and providing the appropriate assurances of confidentiality, two members of our research staff attended the 129 hearings in randomly designated weeks throughout the year. Using forms designed to gather the hearing data, two observers sat in the hearing room recording pertinent information. In some weeks there were no hearings, while in others there were six or seven. No court transcripts were available to us, so the cross-examinations reported below are drawn from the notes the two observers made during the hearings.

The Hearing Room

The hearings at Bellevue and Kings County occurred within the confines of the psychiatric wards. At Bellevue, the hearing room was on the seventh floor of the same building where the psychiatric prison ward occupied the second floor. At Kings County, the hearings took place in the dayroom of the psychiatric prison ward, which was converted each Thursday morning into the hearing room. Both arrangements permitted high security, including barred windows and numerous correction officers.

The hearings at Bellevue took place each Tuesday morning at approximately 10:00 A.M. At about 9:00 A.M. all inmates on the calendar for that day were taken by elevator from the second to the seventh floor and left in a holding room near the hearing room. Across the hall was a place where any friends and relatives attending the hearings waited. The hearing room was a traditional-style courtroom. The judge and court clerk were seated at a bench. Below the bench, the court stenographer worked. To the right of the bench was a seat where the psychiatrists sat when reading their reports and responding to cross-examination. Directly in front of the bench, separated by a railing, was a table. At the middle of the table was a chair for the defendant. To his left was a seat for the defendant's lawyer. To the right, slightly behind the defendant's chair, was a place for relatives or friends of the defendant. At the far right portion of the table was a chair for the district attorney. To the rear were six rows of benches for observers and for staff awaiting upcoming cases.

Each hearing began with the clerk reading the name of the defendant whose hearing was next and a correction officer going to get the defendant. The defendant was seated. If there was some expectation of violence, the correction officer remained standing directly behind the seated defendant; otherwise, he positioned himself near the door. Next, the judge read the psychiatric report. If the report was not contested by the defendant, the judge simply signed the commitment order and moved to the next case. If the defendant or the defendant's attorney did not wish to accept the psychiatric findings, one of the two psychiatrists who carried out the examination and wrote the report would repeat the report. Cross-examination would then take place. In most instances, this cross-examination was done by the defendant's attorney, but occasionally also involved the D.A. In some cases, the defendant was given an opportunity to make a statement after the psychiatrist had finished testifying. Also, when family or friends were present, the judge often invited their comments. Based on all this information, the judge then decided whether the defendant was competent or incompetent. After the decision, the defendant was returned to the waiting room, where he or she remained until all the cases for that day had been heard. Then, the defendants were returned to the psychiatric prison ward to await transfer to a maximum security mental hospital or, if found competent, back to jail for trial.

The setting at Kings County was somewhat different, but the procedures were practically identical. Rather than transferring the defendants from the psychiatric prison ward to a hearing room, the hearing room was brought to the defendants. Each Thursday morning, the dayroom of the prison ward was converted into a hearing room. Tables and chairs were brought in, and the judge, defendants, attorney, and district attorney arranged themselves just as they had at Bellevue, although with less formality than was evident in the traditional courtroom setting there. During the "Son of Sam" hearing, this room was described by a *New York Times* reporter as "a dingy, makeshift courtroom." The district attorney was rarely present at the Kings County hearings. Only if there was something special—a particularly newsworthy case or some unusual legal maneuverings—would a representative of the district attorney be there. The hearings followed the same sequence as Bellevue's hearings.

Overall, the hearings at both locations were highly routinized. All participants knew their places and roles. Since the majority of the defendants involved in the competency hearings were represented by legal aid attorneys, and since the same judges, clerks, and stenographers appeared regularly, the routines hardly varied. As the next section suggests, while there was some variation in the content of the hearings, the routinization of the procedures produced routinized outcomes. Practically all the defendants who had a hearing were found incompetent. Just as the procedures and settings were the same week after week, so, too, were the results.

THE HEARINGS

There are three general types of competency hearings based on whether the psychiatric report is accepted by both parties or is contested. When both the district attorney and the defendant, through his lawyer, accept the psychiatric report, the hearing is referred to as a confirmation. When the defendant or the district attorney wishes to contest the psychiatric findings, the hearing involves the contravening of the submitted report. Each type of hearing has a somewhat different format, and each takes a different amount of time.

Confirmations

Most competency hearings were extremely brief. The client was ushered into the hearing room and nodded to his attorney; the judge read the psychiatric report and asked the attorney if the defendant wished to contest the psychiatric finding of incompetency; the attorney said no; and the judge signed the commitment order. This type of hearing is called a confirmation. Of the 129 hearings attended, 83 (64%) were confirmations. The average length of time for these hearings was four minutes. Even this four-minute figure somewhat overestimates the length of time for confirmations, since 5 of the 83 confirmations took only one minute, 20 required two minutes, and another 20 took only three minutes. Thus, 56 percent of the confirmations lasted three minutes or less. The average comes out to four minutes because one confirmation took 24 minutes, one took 17 minutes, and another 16 minutes. Not only were such lengthy hearings unusual, but also the three longest hearings were protracted over things that had nothing to do with the issue of competency.

The longest confirmation hearing was the very first one under the revised Criminal Procedure Law. It took 24 minutes because of a disagreement between the legal aid attorney and the judge over who should represent the defendant. The legal aid attorney said the lawyer who had represented the defendant in prior adjourned hearings was on vacation and, therefore, the case should be again adjourned until the attorney returned. The district attorney objected, citing many previous adjournments, and insisted that the case be heard that day. The legal aid attorney continued to resist representing the defendants. The judge called his behavior contemptible and termed the defendant's attorney a "shyster." After the judge's outburst, the legal aid attorney agreed to represent the defendant and the hearing routinely proceeded to confirm the psychiatric finding of incompetency. The defendant requested placement in a New York City Veterans Administration hospital, which was not possible under the new statute. Thus, the 24 minutes that elapsed did not raise any substantive questions about competency.

Similarly, the other two long competency hearings did not involve any systematic probing of legal issues. In one, an indictment had been handed up by a grand jury between the time the defendant was admitted for psychiatric evaluation and time of the hearing. Therefore, the arraignment on the recent indictment occurred during the competency hearing. As the arraignment was taking place, the defendant grabbed the indictment and psychiatric reports from the table where the legal aid attorney had placed them and ripped them up. The correction officers moved in quickly and seated the defendant. The confirmation of the psychiatric report proceeded. The third lengthy confirmation hearing occurred during the first week under the revised CPL. It lasted 16 minutes because of the judge's and district attorney's confusion over where the defendant would be sent after the determination of incompetency. Thus, most of the confirmations, which comprised 64 percent of the 129 hearings, were two- or three-minute rubber stampings of the psychiatric reports. There was no serious dialogue on the legal and medical issues.

Defendant Contravening
Not all the competency hearings, however, were confirmations. In 38 of the 129 hearings attended (29%) the defendant disagreed with the psychiatric report. In the language of the court, this is called contravening. One-half of the 38 contravenings dealt exclusively with the issue of the defendant's fitness to proceed with trial. The other 19 dealt fully or partially with dangerousness. Not surprisingly, the hearings in which the psychiatric report was contravened were much longer than the confirmations. The 19 contravenings dealing only with the issue of competency lasted an average of 20 minutes. Those 13 that disputed only the psychiatric finding of dangerousness averaged 18 minutes. Those hearings where both competency and dangerousness were contravened were the longest, averaging 31 minutes.

In 84 percent of the 129 hearings, the attorney for the defendant was a legal aid lawyer, so most of the discussion when the psychiatric reports were contravened came from legal aid attorneys. The major roles in the contravenings were the same as those in the confirmations. The principal difference was that, instead of the judge's simply reading the psychiatric report and signing the commitment order, the psychiatrist took the witness stand, was sworn in, and recapped what was written in the contested report. After this testimony, the psychiatrist was cross-examined by the defendant's attorney and by the district attorney.

Since all our research subjects were declared incompetent to stand trial, the psychiatric testimony was fought unsuccessfully in all cases. For the most part, the cross-examination was perfunctory. In none of the 19 cases were more than five topic areas covered.[1] Most dealt with only one or two areas. Typically, the defense attorney asked for clarification of the symptoms listed on the psychiatric report and questioned the relationship between these symptoms and the defendant's ability to stand trial. Occasionally, there was additional probing about whether a sufficiently comprehensive examination had been carried out, whether the psychiatrist was adequately trained in forensic psychiatry, whether the patient was in a state of remission and thus able to stand trial, or whether the defendant was able to stand trial despite the psychiatric condition.

Just looking at the transcripts of cross-examination of the psychiatrists by the defense attorney is somewhat misleading, however. There was often as much interchange and argument between the judge and attorney as between the psychiatrist and attorney before a resolution was reached. These resolutions often seemed to reflect greater concern with convenient administrative disposition of a case than precise response to medical or legal questions. The kinds of cross-examination and the variety of factors affecting judicial determinations of competency are evident in the following two cases.

The first involved a defendant diagnosed as paranoid schizophrenic who was charged with reckless endangerment and possession of a dangerous weapon. After the psychiatrist read her report, which described the defendant as irrational and not oriented to reality, the judge asked if the defendant had hallucinations. The psychiatrist replied that he did not, that at times he was intact and oriented, but that under strain he had delusions. The district attorney asked the psychiatrist to describe the incident that caused the defendant's arrest. She said that the defendant was sitting on the stoop of his apartment house when the police arrived to arrest him. He allegedly pulled out a pocket knife to protect himself from the police. He did not believe they were police and thought they were trying to kill him and his family. The district attorney then rested his case, and the psychiatrist stepped down from the witness stand.

The legal aid attorney began the questioning of the defendant by asking him who his questioner was. The defendant responded that his questioner was here to defend him. The attorney asked if the defendant was married and if he had children. The defendant replied yes. When asked about the arrest incident, the patient mumbled. The judge asked if the defendant would like to stand to address him. The defendant did. The legal aid attorney asked what the defendant was doing before the police arrived. "Drinking," he answered. The defendant went on to tell how he didn't believe they were police and he was trying to protect himself. The judge asked him whether he felt dizzy or weak. He said he was neither. The judge asked him what he would like him to do. The defendant replied that he wanted him to set bail. The judge then said, "I think you need a little rest before you make your defense." After a pause the judge asked, "What's wrong?" The defendant said, "I'm not guilty." The defendant's attorney interjected, "Do you want to go to a hospital or to court?" "Court," he said. The attorney then asked if the defendant knew what would happen to him if he was returned to court. The defendant said he would have bail set. The attorney asked, "What if you don't get bail?" "I'd rather go to jail than a hospital," responded the defendant.

Following a sharp interchange between the judge and the legal aid attorney, who had objected to a question by the district attorney to the defendant, the judge concluded the hearing by saying, "I'm not declaring you insane. I just want you to stay in a hospital until you're strong enough to defend yourself. I'm not going to send you to court now. I'm going to sign a 90-day order." The hearing was then terminated, after eleven minutes.

The second illustrative case is somewhat atypical because the defendant was represented by a private attorney. This happened in only 16 percent of the 129 cases. However, contrary to our preconceptions, it seemed disadvantageous for most defendants to hire private counsel. In the cases we observed, the private attorneys rarely knew the relevant sections of the Criminal Procedure Law, did not understand the hearing procedures, met with their clients for a shorter time than did the legal aid attorneys, and had almost no knowledge of the mental hygiene facilities to which their clients might be sent. On the other hand, the legal aid lawyers understood the revised statutes (sooner than the judges did, in fact), worked regularly with the relevant statutes, knew the usual operations of the hearings, and understood the implications of the judicial decisions about where their clients would be sent. Overall, it appeared to be in the defendants' best interests to have legal aid attorneys. The defendants received better assistance and it cost less. Also atypical in the second case is that the private attorney was unusually skilled.

In the second case, the private attorney had obtained a second psychiatric opinion in addition to that provided by the Bellevue psychiatrists. This was unusual, but the case itself was typical in its demonstration of how incompetency can be a convenient disposition. The defendant was charged with murder. During the hearing he was groggy, almost asleep. The Bellevue psychiatrist was sworn in and explained that the defendant had been admitted on an emergency admission from the Tombs jail. After his admission, he was put on heavy medication not available in the Tombs. This seemed to be the only reason for his improved mental state. Therefore, the defendant would regress if returned to jail. At the request of a judge at an earlier hearing, the defendant's medication had been reduced. Although the defendant had not been assaultive or acted bizarrely on the lower doses, he still had no appreciation of the charges against him. The Bellevue psychiatrist felt that while the defendant had intellectual knowledge of his charges, he needed a short period of hospitalization to meet the rigors of a trial. In response to an inquiry from the judge, the psychiatrist indicated that the defendant would be competent to stand trial now, except for the medication rules of the New York City Department of Corrections.

The defendant's attorney began his presentation by saying that there was nothing in the Bellevue psychiatrists' testimony to indicate the defendant was incompetent. He called the defendant's private psychiatrist to the stand to testify. The psychiatrist said that he had examined the defendant about six weeks before and that the defendant was without psychosis and could assist in his own defense. The psychiatrist claimed that the defendant accurately gave him the details of the alleged incident in which another man was killed in what appeared to be some sort of "homosexual argument." The psychiatrist certified that the defendant accurately gave a relevant personal history, was appropriate in his moods, suffered from no hallucinations, understood the court procedures, and had integrated ideas that were consistent.

The judge questioned the psychiatrist about the dangerousness issue. He asked whether, if the defendant were returned to the

Tombs for trial, he might not experience additional apprehension. The private psychiatrist said the defendant could absorb that type of threat and was currently in a state of remission. The judge asked if the psychiatrist thought that additional hospitalization could help the defendant. The psychiatrist replied that he did not think that the defendant would be improved over the condition he displayed during his examination, but that an additional period of hospitalization might help.

The judge turned to the attorney and asked if it were true that if the defendant were returned to the Tombs, he would wait about six months before standing trial. The attorney said yes. The judge responded that the defendant would be better off in Bellevue. The district attorney interjected that if the judge found him dangerous, he would go to the correctional maximum security hospital. The judge asked the defendant a series of factual questions about the date and other matters of general orientation. The judge concluded that the defendant was in a state of remission, but if returned to the Tombs would relapse. Therefore, the judge committed the defendant to the Department of Mental Hygiene maximum security hospital for 90 days. The district attorney objected that this finding was contrary to the reports of both psychiatrists. The judge agreed that it was, but he was going to do it anyway.

These examples show some of the common exchanges in the unsuccessful attempts by defendants to contravene psychiatric testimony. In the final section of this chapter, we will examine a few cases that were successfully contravened through more skillful and comprehensive cross-examinations. Because they were found competent, of course, these defendants were not part of our study group.

There is one difference between the Bellevue and the Kings County hearings. At Bellevue, the cross-examination contesting psychiatric findings usually found the psychiatrist on the witness stand and the district attorney supporting the psychiatrist. On the other side was the defendant's attorney. The judge was in the middle, asking questions to clarify or elaborate. At Kings County, the district attorney appeared infrequently. As a result, the judge would often taken the role of the district attorney at the Bellevue hearings by becoming the adversary to the legal aid attorney and the ally of the psychiatrist. The judge seemed forced into this alliance in order to probe adequately the merits of the psychiatrist's report, especially since the legal aid attorney was so proficient in attacking the psychiatrist's testimony. Despite this difference, there was little to distinguish the outcomes of the hearings at the two locations. Approximately the same percentage of cases at both locations involved the defendant's being found incompetent, and about the same proportion of cases involved confirmations.

Noteworthy in discussing the contravened reports was one standard tactic of the legal aid attorneys that appeared to demonstrate a severe conflict of interest. This tactic was to encourage a defendant, after the attorney's initial cross-examination of the psychiatrists, to rise and give a statement. Most often this resulted in groggy, semi-coherent ramblings by the defendants about a wide variety of topics from the illegality of their arrests to their innocence and their need to assault the person who had been spying on them. It thus quickly became apparent that the defendants, who were often on psychotropic medications, were not in touch with much of what was going on around them. The court would then quickly sign the commitment order.

The dilemma that faced legal aid attorneys was whether they were the defendants' guardians or advocates. As a guardian, the attorney would decide what the best course of action for the defendant would be and then do the best he could to obtain this end. As an advocate, the attorney would obtain, to the best of his ability, whatever the defendant wanted, regardless of the attorney's opinion about whether that want was desirable. A solution to this dilemma, used in a number of instances where the attorney felt a defendant was incompetent, but who insisted on disagreeing with the psychiatric report finding him incompetent, was for the attorney to indicate to the court that he was contravening the report. The psychiatrist would then recap the report and there would be perfunctory cross-examination. The defendant would then be invited to make a statement or to question the psychiatrist. The legal aid attorney would sit back and await the inevitable result. The judge would quickly find the defendant incompetent.

District Attorney Contravening

The eight remaining hearings (in addition to the 83 confirmations and 38 patient contravenings) involved objections to the psychiatric report by the district attorney. In four of these seven, the district attorney disagreed with the psychiatrist's finding that a defendant was not dangerous. These hearings averaged 17 minutes, primarily because the district attorney was not familiar with the revised CPL or the Department of Mental Hygiene facility to which the defendants would be sent. In all four cases, the district attorney thought that if the patient were not found dangerous, he or she would be sent to the local state mental hospital, which had a well-earned reputation for patient escapes. While it was true that defendants not found dangerous would be housed in mental hygiene rather than correctional hospitals, during the first six months of the CPL, both agencies shared the same building, the same perimeter security, and the same correction officers.

In the other four cases in which the district attorney objected to the court proceedings, the defendant wished to confirm the psychiatric finding of incompetency, but the district attorney wanted an adjournment so that an indictment could be obtained before the determination of incompetence. Again, the district attorney was concerned that unless the defendant was indicted first, no decision had to be made about dangerousness, and thus the defendant would necessarily be committed to a mental hygiene hospital rather than the well-known correctional hospital. Although this was true, the level of security was the same at both facilities. In all four cases, the court refused the district attorney's request for an adjournment because of numerous prior adjournments and because of assurances of high security provided by the mental hygiene facility.

In sum, the majority (64%) of the competency hearings routinely accepted the psychiatric report finding the defendant incompetent. In 29 percent of the hearings, the patients disagreed with the psychiatric findings to no avail. These hearings were somewhat less routine. The legal aid or private attorneys questioned the psychiatrists with varying effectiveness and aggressiveness. In a small number of cases (6%), the district attorney, because of confusion about the revised statutes, pressed either for adjournments, which were not granted, or for findings of dangerousness where the psychiatric report determined the defendant not to be dangerous. Because of the repetitious subject matter and because the same attorneys, district attorneys, judges, and psychiatrists participated each week, the hearings went very smoothly, with standard routines and predictable outcomes. However, as we shall discuss in the next section, not all the hearings ended with a finding of incompetency.

This section has described only the 129 hearings that involved members of our study group. Because this group was, by definition, a group of incompetent felony defendants, these data describe hearings that ended with a determination of incompetency. Almost all hearings do, but some do not. We now discuss these few to round out the picture of competency hearings.

HEARINGS WHERE THE DEFENDANT WAS FOUND COMPETENT
During twenty-six weeks of data collection, we observed 12 hearings involving felony defendants found incompetent by the examining psychiatrists, but determined competent by the court. In only 8 percent (12) of the 141 cases observed, did the court disagree with the psychiatrists. This agreement rate of 92 percent is amazingly comparable to a number of studies of civil commitment hearings, where the agreement rate of judges and psychiatrists was between 90 and 100 percent (Miller and Schwartz 1966; Wegner and Fletcher 1969). The courts, both civil and criminal, very rarely disagree with the psychiatric recommendations they receive.

As might be expected, the hearings that were successfully contravened were much longer than most others. They averaged twenty-two minutes. One hearing took one hour and six minutes to complete. One working hypothesis was that these cases involved less serious charges. However, this did not appear to be accurate. Although complete information on those defendants found competent was not available to us, the data collected during the hearings on the defendants who successfully contravened showed that their offenses included a knife assault on a father and two friends, a burglary, and an assault on a waitress. In most instances something in the merits of the case combined with an especially sound cross-examination by the defendant's attorney to produce the successful contravention. The major factor in the success of these contravenings was a particularly skillful legal aid attorney at Kings County, where 8 of the 12 successful contravenings occurrred.

One case involved a defendant charged with third degree burglary whose symptoms were diagnosed as coming from some somatic or psychotic reaction. The psychiatrist testified that there were indications the defendant was malingering, that is, "faking it," but he had been so successful at convincing himself that he had a thought disorder that this prevented him from meeting the competency standards. The defendant was described as having the disorder imbedded in his unconscious and as being unable to help himself out of this condition. He was diagnosed as having "Gans Syndrome" as a result of being imprisoned. In the cross-examination, it came out that he had never communicated with the examining psychiatrist.

Following this psychiatric testimony, the defendant was sworn in and, under the direction of the legal aid attorney, talked for about five minutes about the circumstances of his arrest and detention. When asked why he had remained mute to the hospital psychiatrists, the defendant replied that he would talk only to his counsel. The judge asked the psychiatrist if, based on the testimony he had heard, he would change his mind. The psychiatrist said yes, noting that the court had just observed the spontaneous remission of the psychiatric condition that had prevented the defendant from standing trial.

Another cased involved a defendant charged with assaulting a waitress in a restaurant. After the psychiatrist was sworn in, he gave the dates of his two examinations of the defendant. He had concluded that the defendant was incompetent because of a long history of psychiatric illness; because he was currently out of contact with reality; because he was not able to understand his legal predicament; and because, as a result, he could not assist in his defense. The legal aid attorney asked what the psychiatrist meant by a "psychotic thought disorder." The psychiatrist said that the defendant was not able to organize his thoughts or to understand situations. The legal aid attorney inquired if the defendant knew where he was arrested. The psychiatrists replied yes, but cited some irrelevant comments the defendant had made about having $50 in Chinese money and other statements that had no contextual validity.

After this testimony, the defendant took the stand. His attorney asked him to recount what had happened just before his arrest. The defendant said the waitress would not wait on him, became frightened, and called the police. He continued to insist on being waited on, then tried to pay the waitress and leave. The defendant claimed that it was a case of false arrest. The legal aid attorney said that he felt the defendant was capable of standing

trial. The judge asked if the defendant had the capacity to produce witnesses for a trial. The attorney said yes. The judge said
that he was not sure on either count. The legal aid attorney
responded that the defendant had had trouble before in this
restaurant and that this may have contributed to his present
arrest. The attorney continued, stating that while the defendant
might be in need of psychiatric help, he was competent to stand
trial. The judge agreed and the defendant was returned to court
to stand trial.

These two cases, and the other ten where the court disagreed
with the psychiatric reports, give some indication that there are
many complexities involved in determining competency. However, the few disagreements between the psychiatrists and the
courts also indicate how much this legal decision is based on a
straight medical decision. For the most part, the competency
hearings supported, after routine and cursory reviews, the psychiatric reports. What is crucial in a defendant's being found incompetent is the psychiatric evaluation. In our data, when the
psychiatrists decided a defendant was incompetent, there was a
92 percent certainty that the court would agree.

We have described some of the procedures and complexities of
the determination of incompetency. Now we can examine how
this diversion from the criminal justice system affects the disposition of the charges against the defendants and the speed of their
return to the community. These are the crucial questions that the
next two chapters address. Under what hospital conditions were
these incompetent defendants detained? How did the defendants
perceive these conditions relative to the alternatives of jail and
prison? How many defendants actually returned to trial? How
many were convicted and sentenced? How does the total length of
time detained in mental hospitals and prisons compare with that
for convicted defendants who were not found incompetent?

5   Maximum Security Detention
Facilities

In 1966 filmmaker Frederick Wiseman pro-
duced the controversial and frightening film *Titicut Follies,* which
portrays the horrors of a maximum security hospital for the
criminally insane. This film graphically showed the force-feeding
of a patient who had refused to eat, naked patients in seclusion
rooms, and an apparently rational person detained pretrial for
three years on a minor property offense for reasons that his
psychiatrist could barely elucidate. The depiction of terrifying
institutional oppressiveness was highlighted by the black and
white photography. The film was shot at Bridgewater State Hospital, Massachusetts's maximum security facility for defendants
incompetent to stand trial. *Titicut Follies* was so powerful and
controversial that a court order was obtained to prevent its showing
in Massachusetts.

Rather than the dismal, frightening picture Wiseman made of
Bridgewater, the pictures typically drawn by district attorneys
and held by the public of the institutions that house incompetent
defendants are more like the facility described in the *New York
Times* on November 1, 1977. The hospital described was Creedmoor Psychiatric Center, one of the 28 regular civil hospitals in
the New York State system. Creedmoor was picked because the

assistant district attorney from Queens noted, "What troubles me is that Berkowitz could be transferred here one day. Since most of the Son of Sam killings took place in Queens he may come under our jurisdiction. I wouldn't want to see him in there with those open gates." The article discusses in great detail how defendants who are incompetent to stand trial or acquitted by reason of insanity end up in hospitals where "there are at least as many ways of going out as coming in, and there is a great deal of casual two-way traffic. The dozen or so exits vary from open gates to bent bars, tree limbs reaching out to freedom and picnic tables stacked together next to the eight foot fence."

This *New York Times* article spells out in great detail the hospital procedures that permit patients to eat at nearby diners and utilize parks in the vicinity of the hospital. The reporter's point is that "The interplay of state law and psychiatric practice has produced a system that often enables a criminally insane individual to make his way back to society and the streets, sometimes within a year or two, through a number of different routes, without much difficulty." The public is presented with a picture of the detention facilities for incompetent defendants and other types of criminally committed mental patients that supports their worst fears.

Similar concerns characterized the four cases discussed in chapter 4, in which the district attorney contravened the psychiatric reports that did not find a defendant dangerous. The district attorney contended that the defendants, if not found dangerous and housed in the maximum security correctional hospital, would find their way to a mental hygiene facility from which they could easily escape, and thereby avoid prosecution. In a similar vein, during one of the cases where the defendant was contravening the psychiatric findings of incompetency, the judge told him that he would get a good rest by going up to the "Matteawan campus." The judge's phrase suggested a bucolic setting where the tensions of city life could be worked out within the confines of a large open space and casual atmosphere.

When the depictions of mental hospitals for incompetent defendents offered by judges, district attorneys, and the *New York Times* are compared with those of *Titicut Follies,* the contrast is rather startling. Is the institutional life of the incompetent defendant one of freedom to wander around a campus with ready access to community recreation and escape, or is it one of oppressive, inhumane constraint characterized by naked bodies in seclusion cells controlled by restrictive, unsympathetic psychiatrists? The answers are critical in determining whether incompetent defendants are indeed "beating a rap." The implication of many news reports is that mental health diversion for alleged offenders allows them to avoid the harsh realities of prisons and to return much more quickly to the street. This chapter deals with the realities of maximum security mental hospital confinement for the 539 incompetent defendants we followed. The question of how quickly they returned to the community will be the focus of chapter 6.

How do the facilities that house these incompetent defendants compare with prisons and jails? How oppressive and dehumanizing are these maximum security hospitals? How frequent is physical and mental brutality? What do secure mental hospitals look like? Do the incompetent defendants actually prefer being in these mental hospitals to being in other hospitals or jail?

These questions will be answered based on (1) observations made by five white middle-class researchers who paid weekly visits for nearly two years to the maximum security facilities where the 539 incompetent defendants were sent and (2) on data gathered through structured interviews with these defendants. The interviews were of two types. First, defendants were interviewed during the week prior to their discharge from the maximum security facilities. These were called pretransfer interviews. Some of these defendants were returning to jail and impending trials; some were being transferred to other state civil hospitals; a few were being released outright because their criminal charges had been dropped and they were no longer deemed in need of care and treatment. Of the 539 defendants, 341 (63%) were successfully interviewed. The remaining 198 were not interviewed for a variety of reasons. During the first six months, while procedures to interview the defendants confidentially were being developed, no correctional hospital transfers were included in our survey. Of the Department of Mental Hygiene transfers not interviewed, most were missed because the hospital did not notify us enough in advance that the defendants were to be transferred—and also because of a few refusals.

In addition to these pretransfer interviews, other data relevant to the defendants' perceptions of these maximum security facilities were gathered from a series of interviews done at five different times with all residents of the mental hygiene maximum security facility. These interviews focused on patients' attitudes toward attempts to change the facility from a purely custodial to a more therapeutic model. These data are reported in detail elsewhere (Steadman, Cocozza, and Lee 1978). However, as part of these interviews, some data were obtained pertaining to the questions of this chapter. Four hundred thirty-eight interviews were completed among the 539. Some individuals who were retained for longer times were interviewed two or three times over an 18-month period.

Three different institutions were used to house the defendants after they were found incompetent. This occurred because of the political climate and administrative machinations surrounding the implementation of the Criminal Procedure Law that required the Department of Mental Hygiene to care for all incompetent defendants, except those found dangerous. Despite having decided to care for these defendants at a single centralized state facility, DMH had no such facility available. Thus, in September, 1971, five months after the state of New York had for the first time in its history laid off state workers, funds were being sought to establish a maximum security hospital within DMH. Because of fiscal constraints between September, 1971, and March, 1972, the defendants under Mental Hygiene auspices were housed on wards within the Matteawan State Hospital. Matteawan was the Department of Correctional Services' maximum security hospital for dangerous incompetent defendants. Thus, the setting for the first six months was a traditional corrections maximum security hospital.

In March, 1972, the Department of Mental Hygiene took over a refurbished building within the perimeter security of Matteawan, but distinct from the building they had previously shared with Corrections. Until January, 1973, the defendants remained in this building, called Mid-Hudson because of its location about midway down the Hudson River between Albany and New York City. In January, 1973, after ten months in the Mid-Hudson building, all the defendants were moved to another refurbished facility in New Hampton, New York. This move totally separated the Mental Hygiene maximum security hospital, Mid-Hudson, from Matteawan. Therefore, questions about the conditions under which the incompetent defendants were detained will be examined in three sections. Each phase of the institution's development reflects the attempt to move from a custodial corrections model to a more therapeutic model.

This examination of detention conditions in three distinct types of maximum security institutions provides some sense of the range of facilities that exist across the U.S. In states like New York and California, incompetent defendants have been cared for in hospitals run entirely by departments of corrections. In other states, such as Massachusetts and Iowa, the facilities for incompetent defendants are run jointly by departments of mental health and corrections, often with Mental Health providing funds and treatment and Corrections contributing the internal and perimeter security staff. This joint operation characterized the Mid-Hudson building within the Matteawan perimeter security. Finally, some states, such as North Carolina and Tennessee, charge mental health departments with the full responsibility for both treatment and security. This is now true in New York State. This model became operative when the Mid-Hudson Psychiatric Center moved to New Hampton in January, 1973.

As the model for maximum security detention moves toward emphasizing the treatment modalities of a department of mental health in conjunction with maximum security, it may become a more attractive alternative than the traditional hospital for the criminally insane, where the inmates receive what has been called "the worst of both worlds." Surely the institution presented in *Titicut Follies* offered practically nothing that was preferable to prison. However, the state mental hospital written up in the *New York Times* just as surely offers much that is preferable to prison. Overall, as will become clear, the facilities that now detain most incompetent defendants are at some point midway between these two extremes.

THE CORRECTIONS MODEL

From September 13, 1971, through March 23, 1972, all incompetent felony defendants, dangerous or not, were housed in Matteawan State Hospital. Those that were dangerous were completely under Correction Department auspices. The others were housed on designated wards with medical services provided by Mental Hygiene Department employees. However, security was provided by the same correction officers used elsewhere in Matteawan. This arrangement reflected the problems of establishing a maximum security institution at a time of severe fiscal austerity. The New York State Department of Mental Hygiene was instructed by the Division of the Budget to provide the physical structure and staff with its existing allocations. The theory was that with a continuing decrease in the number of psychiatric inpatients in all state mental facilities, existing funds could be used to set up this new program. As a result, there was no appropriate DMH facility ready when the CPL became effective on September 1, 1971. Therefore, psychiatrists, correction officers, and space were purchased from Matteawan. The detention of incompetent defendants during this period was almost entirely within a traditional correctional model.

Matteawan was among the first state facilities earmarked for the detention of the criminally insane. It was established in 1892 to house incompetent defendants and convicted inmates in need of psychiatric services. Its red-brick, turretted buildings sit atop a hill in rich, rural farm land, conjuring up the image of a thunderstorm on a black night, complete with mad scientists. It is surrounded by a sixteen-foot chainlink fence illuminated by spotlights and watched by correction officers. There is little question that it is a prison. Matteawan and the Department of Correction's other mental hospital were described as places where "there always lurks the grisly possibility that a prisoner... will be marooned and foresaken" (*U.S. ex. Rel. Schuster* v. *Herold,* 410 Federal Reporter, 2d10719 [1969]).

The same judge also said that "by its very nature, confinement at an institution for the criminally insane is far more restrictive than at a prison." Thus, one might expect that, contrary to some press and popular conceptions, detention facilities operating on the corrections model might not be very desirable alternatives for defendants looking for easy ways out of the prison system.

Physically, the buildings in which the Department of Mental Hygiene set up its programs were identical with those of Corrections. The correction officers were the same as those who worked on the correction wards during their regular hours. However, there were some attempts to alter the environment on the two wards that fell under DMH. The physical arrangement of the wards used during these first six months was the same as that of the corrections portion of the hospital. There was a large, open room, where each patient had a bed. A dayroom had a television set, a couple of tables, and twenty or so chairs. Near the center of each ward was the desk area, where the correction officers spent most of their time. From there they could see the entire dayroom. The patients were required to stay in the dayroom except for an hour after lunch, when all patients were required to take naps.

The daily routine was unvarying. After getting up at 6:30 A.M., there was time to wash before the count that preceded breakfast. All patients were lined up, counted, and moved into the dining area for breakfast. After breakfast, they were returned to the wards, where they received medication, hung around, watched T.V., mopped floors, collected or distributed laundry, and so forth, until lunch. At approximately 11:30, another count was taken. Patients then proceeded to lunch. After lunch, there was the required one-hour nap and then more hanging around until the shift changed at 2:30 P.M. and another count was taken. At 4:30, the dinner count was taken and dinner served in the dining area. Patients had free time until lights-out at 9:30 P.M. Some patients would go out to work details elsewhere in the hospital or have brief visits off the wards with psychiatrists interspersed with these routines. At this stage, however, there was no active treatment except for the medication.

The issues that arose during this initial period of takeover by Mental Hygiene from Corrections centered on uncertainties of the correction officers about what, if any, additional rights patients had under DMH rather than Corrections auspices. When we and the assistant commissioner in charge of the facility visited the hospital in its second day of operation, the correction officers pummeled him with questions about whether the patients were allowed to have matches; when visitors would be allowed; how they should handle contraband; what to do about medical emergencies, since the Mental Hygiene patients were not permitted to use the Matteawan infirmary (which belonged to Corrections); and what type of light switches they were going to have on the wards. The conflicts between DMH and corrections policies were evident. In Correction facilities, for example, inmates were not allowed to have matches, but on the closed wards in DMH hospitals, unless the patients had shown previous indications of arson, they were permitted to have matches. Likewise, most DMH hospitals had regular light switches that anyone could operate, while Correction Department facilities had special switches requiring a key to operate to prevent the inmates from adjusting the lights themselves.

The impression of a lack of any meaningful differences between the Corrections and Mental Hygiene wards in Matteawan was reinforced when we talked informally with the correction officers on the DMH wards two weeks after the facility opened. When we inquired what they thought the differences were between these two parts of the hospital, they mentioned only the shower schedule and the use of matches. The DMH patients were allowed to shower only three times a week, rather than once a day, as in "the rest of Matteawan." While the patients were allowed to have matches, the correction officers were pushing to have cigarette lighters built into the walls, so that patients would not have matches or lighters in their personal possession. They mentioned nothing about any noticeable differences in the treatment programs.

Later, we received one indication from the correction officers about a difference between the two programs. One of the ward charges during the first month felt that doctors were more often on the ward run by DMH than had been true on the Corrections side. The Matteawan situation was typified by his description of one doctor, "He shows up, signs in in the book and then doesn't want to see any patients. [During] a month he doesn't see the patients assigned to him for more than five seconds." In addition to having more doctors working in the DMH portion, the ward charge also thought the patients were easier to manage because in Matteawan there were no privileges that could be rescinded and no program that could be taken away as punishment. He implied that there were some privileges in the Department of Mental Hygiene wards that could be.

During the first four months of observing and talking with patients and staff on the Mental Hygiene wards in Matteawan, there were some indications that not only was the DMH side not better, but in some ways it was worse. Six weeks after the facility opened, we were given a tour of the library area. It contained twenty-five or thirty dog-eared books. The two most recent copyright dates that we could find were 1936 and 1940. During this same visit, we were informed that during this, the sixth week of the Mental Hygiene presence, the patients were being permitted into the yard for the first time. For the first six weeks, not a single patient on the DMH side got any outdoor exercise, whereas such opportunities were daily occurrences on most Matteawan wards. One of the staff psychiatrists lamented in January, 1972, that there were almost no activities open to the patients except watching television. Later in the same visit to the wards, the ward charge commented that there were movies once a week, but instead of scheduling them for the evening, when the patients were particularly bored and there were no visitors, movies were shown on Friday mornings, a bad time because this was prime time for patients to see doctors.

Some positive differences between the Corrections and Mental Hygiene parts of Matteawan in the first two months subsequently disappeared. For instance, on October 5, when we were brought through the Matteawan wards to reach the DMH wards, we noted that all the patients in the dayroom of one ward were watching television, playing cards, sitting, or sleeping. Since sleeping was not allowed in the dormitory area during the day, four patients were asleep on the floor under tables and two were asleep slouched in chairs. Patients on the DMH wards were not as highly sedated, and none were seen sleeping on the floors. However, one month later, on November 8, 1971, we observed for the first time two patients sleeping on the floor of a DMH ward. We also noted that the standard Matteawan practice of the correction officer's yelling "seats" upon the entrance of a visitor to the wards to indicate that all the patients must sit down and not walk around, was now heralding our presence. It had not two months previous.

Just as there were a variety of such indicators suggesting a similarity of the DMH and Corrections operations, so, too, one of the typical prison issues, guard brutality toward the patients, grew to be a constant issue in our discussions with patients and staff. The first indication that this was to be one of the main recurring issues throughout our research came in October, 1971. We were talking with one of the correction officers in his office when one of the patients came in and said to him, "Do you want Fishman in a jacket?"[1] The officer said that he did. The patients proceeded to get a camisole (straight-jacket) and put Fishman into it without incident. The officer turned to us and said that the patients help around the wards in a lot of ways like that—with laundry, making coffee, and the like.

Two weeks later we were talking with a group of patients on the ward when one patient complained that "there is no therapy here and smacking a guy around is no way to conduct a program." When asked what he meant, he alleged that the correction officers get certain patients to put other patients into camisoles and encourage the patients to "work them over" in the process. In this way the correction officers, he alleged, could keep their hands clean and yet see that patients were punished for their misbehavior.

In a similar vein, the issue of staff brutality and devious means of covering it up arose during one of our pretransfer interviews. One of the patients who had been on the ward nearly since its beginning complained that there were not enough towels on the ward for the patients. He claimed that enough towels were allocated, but that the correction officers kept most of them to wrap around their fists in order to avoid leaving incriminating marks and to keep from hurting their hands when they hit patients. A second patient complained of the same problem in an informal discussion. Both patients were angry not so much at the staff's alleged brutality, but because they wanted more towels.

Leaving the wards one day, we proceeded through the dining area when one DMH ward was at lunch. The officers and patients from the ward did not see us come into the dining area. As we walked through, we saw an officer confront a patient who was strapped into a camisole and seated at one of the tables and yell abusively, "Fishman, when the fuck are you going to straighten out?" The correction officers who saw us grinned broadly, apparently acknowledging that we had inadvertently seen a typical officer-patient interaction.

The issue of the use of jackets for disciplinary purposes rather than as protective devices became heated in January, 1972. It reflected some of the growing tension between the correction officers, who felt the psychiatrists were soft on security, and the psychiatrists who had been hired by DMH to establish a treatment program within the maximum security facility. The psychiatric position was that camisoles were to be used only for brief periods when patients required restraint from hitting other patients and staff or when patients seriously threatened suicide. The correction officers tended to employ the camisole as a punishment for any infringement of ward rules or for talking back to the officers. In January, 1972, the DMH hospital director required that a patient who had been placed in seclusion by the officer on duty be released. The officers felt that such questioning of their authority weakened the security they could provide. The incident highlighted some of the developing tensions produced by mental hygiene philosophies in these security-oriented facilities.[2]

Actually, the issues of the inappropriate use of camisoles reached a head after our data collection had ended. A consent order was issued by a U.S. district court in July, 1976, in response to a civil suit, *Negron* v. *Ward* (74 Civ. 1480), as a result of a petition filed in May, 1974, by Valentine Negron, a patient in Matteawan, against the group of correction officers. The patients contended that they were subjected to cruel and unusual punishment by the excessive use of seclusion and restraints. In the court's consent order, the Departments of Correctional Services and Mental Hygiene agreed that "an inmate shall not be placed in restraint or seclusion simply because his presence on his normal housing ward is disruptive to the correctional staff or to other inmates." Also, agreement was reached that "any time that an examining physician orders that a Matteawan inmate be placed or continued in restraint or seclusion, a detailed statement of the examining physician's clinical observations of the patient shall be maintained, including the patient's physical condition, apparel, overt behavior, and mental status, a statement of the physician's reason for initiating or continuing the seclusion procedure; and a statement of his treatment plan shall be maintained." Thus, through this court action, all parties involved in the care and detention of the incompetent felony defendant admitted the abuses that we had observed, and the tensions between traditional correctional approaches and more therapeutic programs were clearly evident.

Overall, our observations and discussions during the six months that the DMH patients were housed on wards within Matteawan suggested that initially there may have been some differences between the Corrections and Mental Hygiene programs, but most of these faded away after a few weeks when no programs were developed. Some of the ugly incidents depicted in Frederick Wiseman's *Titicut Follies* were absent, but the restrictiveness of the facility and the indications of physical brutality suggested little reason for these defendants to prefer where they were to being in prison. In fact, the interviews with 52 patients who were transferred out of the DMH wards during these six months, and with 57 others who spent all their time on the Matteawan correctional wards throughout the entire research, provide some indications that the defendants themselves had no desire to beat their raps by being where they were.

Unfortunately, the interviews done in the Mid-Hudson portion of Matteawan did not generate much data directly addressing these issues because of the interview schedule that was originally designed to be used throughout the research. Initially, this interview contained eight open-ended questions tapping defendants' impressions of Mid-Hudson, what they expected to happen after they left the facility, and the stigma that might be attached to being a patient there. Questions directly related to the desirability or undesirability of being there were developed only in later drafts of the interview schedule. Interviews with the patients in the Correction portion of Matteawan were more comprehensive and more comparable to the later interviews at Mid-Hudson.

The interviews in the Mid-Hudson wards showed that the Mental Hygiene patients felt more negatively about their situation than did the patients in the Correction wards. Asked what they thought about Mid-Hudson, only 38 percent indicated that it was good, 42 percent said it was lousy, and 20 percent had mixed reactions. Yet, despite the negative impressions our observers had when walking through the Matteawan wards, 60 percent of the patients interviewed just prior to their transfers back to court from Matteawan indicated that they thought Matteawan was either excellent or good. Thirty-six percent said it was lousy, and 4 percent had mixed reactions.

Our initial reaction to these results was that the difference between the interview data and our observations might be related to the more serious criminal charges against the defendants in Matteawan, compared with the charges against those in Mid-Hudson. Had the Matteawan patients been indicted on their criminal charges, it might have been more advantageous to them to avoid convictions and long prison sentences by diversion into a mental hospital than it was for the Mid-Hudson patients, who generally faced less serious charges. However, the responses of the Mid-Hudson and the Matteawan defendants showed no statistically significant differences in how positive the defendants felt based on how serious were the criminal charges that they faced. Those facing violent crimes against persons were as likely not to like Matteawan or Mid-Hudson as were those facing property crime charges.

The only reason we could find for the apparently more negative attitudes toward Mid-Hudson, which appeared preferable to Matteawan to our observers, was the higher expectations that the patients had about Mid-Hudson when they were told upon being found incompetent that they were being transferred to a Mental Hygiene facility. Prior to the Criminal Procedure Law, this would have meant transfer to a regular security civil hospital. For the first six months after the implementation of the CPL, the "Mental Hygiene facility" was simply several wards within Matteawan, an institution well-known to inmates in the state prison system. One patient who had previously been in Matteawan said that he was very upset when he saw the car that was delivering him come through the Matteawan gates and pull up in front of a building in which he had been before. Because the patients had expected things to be easier in a Mental Hygiene than a Corrections facility, they were not happy with what they found.

Despite the higher level of favorable response among Matteawan patients compared with the Mid-Hudson patients, there were clear indications that the defendants in Matteawan would have preferred to be in another mental hospital rather than the one in which they found themselves. Asked if they would rather be in Matteawan or another hospital, 40 of the 50 patients who responded said they would rather be in another hospital. Their responses to this question should not necessarily be taken to indicate that the defendants in Matteawan would prefer to be in jail awaiting trial to being in Matteawan. In fact, when asked whether they would rather be in Matteawan or in jail, only 19 of the 51 respondents (34%) picked jail.

In sum, responses toward Mid-Hudson were less positive than had been anticipated from observations on the wards. The discrepancy seemed related to the higher expectations held by defendants sent to Mental Hygiene for a somewhat easier existence and their disappointment at finding a maximum security facility that was practically the same as the Corrections mental hospital. What may have appeared to be an easy way out was not. However, the Mental Hygiene program for incompetent defendants did not remain in Matteawan throughout our research. It moved to another location in March, 1972. In this next phase it became a greater mix of Mental Hygiene and Corrections, and the tension between treatment and security emerged even more sharply.

THE MIXED MENTAL HYGIENE-CORRECTIONAL MODEL

To develop a more therapeutic environment for the incompetent defendants under its auspices, DMH refurbished a three-story building within the perimeter security of Matteawan. It was felt that physical separation was essential to break away from what was seen as the purely custodial detention of Matteawan. A psychologist was added to the treatment staff, as were two social workers and a recreational specialist.

When the Mental Hygiene operation was shifted to Mid-Hudson, major changes were made. The shift of the 112 patients in Mid-Hudson occurred in March, 1972, after six months in the Matteawan wards. The field notes of one observer make clear the striking contrast between the Mid-Hudson building and Matteawan.

We were impressed with the spaciousness and the almost finished state of the place. The entire second floor is almost ready. The plumbing and painting have been completed and there is about another day or two of electrical work to be completed. There are about 30 single or double rooms on each wing. Almost all are equipped with beds and lockers. The hallways are wide, the colors are refreshing, and there is plenty of window space... There are two large courtyards enclosed by the L-shaped wings of the building. The whole thing is a striking contrast to Mid-Hudson's present living quarters.

The L-shape of the wards was a significant change for the correction officers who remained as the ward staff at Mid-Hudson. Rather than having a large dayroom on one side of the ward and the sleeping area on the other side, the officers were faced with providing security for areas that they could not see from behind their desk. Furthermore, instead of a large dormitory area, each ward had 20 to 30 rooms with one to four beds. Not only could they not easily see all ends of the hallways from their desks, but they could see almost none of the sleeping areas. For them this raised problems in dealing with patient fights and homosexual activity, activities sometimes interrelated.

While there was substantial disapproval for this new arrangement among the officers, for the patients it was a godsend. The

notes written by two observers who visited Mid-Hudson the day
that the first patients were moved capture the patients' feelings:

It appeared as though there was euphoria on the ward. They
[the patients] were extremely happy. The level of activity on the
ward was amazing. It was like a bunch of kids moving into a
college dormitory three days before registration. They were
making beds, they were walking, they were literally bounding
around. Only about 10 of the forty were watching TV and only six
or so of them were really engrossed in the TV, the others were just
sitting in that general area. The rest of the ward was setting up
the beds' headboards which had recently come in, or were visiting
each other or were talking in the rooms. Some hadn't been there
more than a couple of hours and were still moving in their own
belongings. This was really a sight to see because the contrast
between 21 [the previous ward] even after it had been painted
after the fire and 4 and 15 [two other correction wards] to this
ward was just amazing.

The *ward is bright,* wide open, plenty of space, and very
refreshing looking compared to the old building. The patients are
extremely happy about being there. When we walked in, one
patient came running over to me to tell me that he didn't want to
go back to court now; he wanted to do his one year commitment right here. He then went dancing off snapping his fingers.
Everything we saw pointed to the same thing—the patients really
like it over there. They were putting beds together and bringing
equipment upstairs and they really seemed to enjoy having
something to do. Just about all of them were beaming, inter-
acting with each other more than ever, and full of energy. You
would have never guessed you were in a mental hospital.

The officers didn't look so happy. When we asked them how
they liked it there, all we got was a shrug of the shoulders or "I
don't know." They didn't seem at all willing to talk about it.
Their reaction struck me as one of cautious indifference. The
place is laid out in such a way that the patients have room to move
around and are out of sight of the officers, at least momentarily.
It is very unlike what these officers are used to.

Things quieted down fairly rapidly, and more sedate routines
were established. Three days after the initial transfer of patients,
however, the following observations were recorded.

All 112 patients were transferred to the new building as of the
morning of March 26. Things had settled down considerably

since we were there on Thursday. Things still appeared to be
considerably more pleasant, enthusiastic and active than in the
old building but the chaos and euphoria evident on Thursday had
leveled off considerably. There is a considerable amount of
sleeping which continues to take place throughout the day. I
would estimate on Ward 1 that about 15 out of the 56 patients
were sleeping at any one time during the course of the day. This is
a privilege which they did not have in the old building, except
immediately after lunch, if they chose to sleep they had to do it
either on the floor or in a chair whereas in the new building they
can go to their room and sleep any time they want. There was
more card playing going on, each ward had a Monopoly game
which was in use almost the entire time we were on the ward. It
was being used as a Monopoly game about 2/3's of that time, the
rest of that time the money and dice were being used to play craps
by a few of the patients. There is considerably less TV watching
going on. On Tuesday morning for example, there were only two
patients who were really watching although another five were
sitting around in the same general area. This contrasts markedly
with the old building where on [ward] 15 when of about 50
patients, you would get anywhere from 10 to 15 at any given point
in time watching TV.

These positive changes did not mean that some of the issues
and problems noted about the Matteawan wards did not persist.
Conflicts continued between the psychiatrists directing the Mid-
Hudson program and the correction officers. Three days after the
patient transfers had been completed, on a Sunday night, a
patient picked up a mop wringer and threw it through a window.
The officers put him into seclusion. On Monday morning, when
the psychiatrists read the officer's report, they released the patient
from seclusion. When we arrived late on Monday morning, the
officer was very upset. He felt that the doctors' overruling him
weakened his authority in the eyes of the patients and made
officers more liable to attack. In his view, they were now less able
to provide adequate security.

The most significant problem other than the treatment-security
issue related to brutality. In the first few weeks at the new
building, little was mentioned about this. In fact, in early April,
one of the officers escorting us to the ward for our weekly visit
complained about the placidity of Mid-Hudson compared to
Matteawan. He said, "It is too quiet over here. Nothing [in the

way of fights] happens." Another officer said that, "There's never any action over here." However, as the program became more settled, the conflict between Corrections and Mental Hygiene approaches to the patients became evident.

In July, a correction officer complained that he did not know what was expected of him by Mental Hygiene. He cited two examples that had occurred while he was acting charge on the ward. The first involved a patient who was running around the ward nude and was therefore put in a camisole. Later that day, while out in the yard, one of the other patients helped him out of the jacket. Naked, he attempted to scale the fence. This officer said he attempted to find out who had helped the patient out of the jacket by punching a patient a couple of times in the stomach. He was unsuccessful in obtaining the information. The officer later was admonished by his supervisor who said, "This is Mental Hygiene and you can't punish patients." The supervisor said that the patients were sick and should not be hit. The officer relating the story said that he had worked for Corrections for four years and did not understand how you could control patients if hitting them was not permitted.

In the second incident, the officer found in a bathroom a pen top melted into a sharp nail. This precipitated a shakedown of the ward. During the shakedown, a pillowcase containing a rock was found inside the wall of a room. The patient who had moved into the room that day was put into seclusion, even though there was no way of determining whether this contraband had been hidden by the room's previous or current occupant. Again, the officer was overridden by his supervisor, who released the patient from seclusion. The officer summed up his long description of these two incidents by asking, "If you can't punish a guy, how are you supposed to relate to him?"

The use of camisoles and seclusion for punishment rather than for deterrence and the conflicts between the officers' previous set of rules and those of Mid-Hudson were evident in two incidents we observed directly. The first occurred about four weeks after the transfers to the new building. A patient was quietly watching television. For no apparent reason, another patient walked up to him and began yelling at him. To keep the yelling patient away, the patient who had been sitting rose and picked up the fiberglass chair on which he had been sitting. He then put the

chair down, swung, and hit the yelling patient on the cheek. At
this point two officers rushed in and broke up the scuffle. The
officers decided to put both patients into jackets to punish this
violation of acceptable ward behavior. Both patients stood quietly
while put into the camisoles.

One month later we observed four patients on one ward in
camisoles and asked the officer why. He said they had been found
with contraband during a recent shakedown of the ward. All the
patients had been bartering medication which had been given
them, but which they had not taken. The patients had not resisted
being put into the camisoles because they also felt that this
punishment was normal for such infractions.

Another illustrative incident occurred in early July, 1972. While
we were there one of the patients yelled, cursed, and screamed at
the officers and the supervisors passing through the ward. The officers appeared to be very frustrated in their attempts to verbally
subdue the patient. Eventually, they did calm him down by
talking to him. As the observers were escorted from the ward
after finishing some interviews, someone commented to the officer that they seemed to be having a little trouble with the
patient. The officer replied that they had been specifically told to
go easy on that patient because he was getting out soon and
therefore should not be put in seclusion. He continued, "I would
have slammed him a few if there weren't visitors [us] on the
ward . . ."

Patient-patient and staff-patient violence were regular topics
of conversation during our discussions with the correction officers
and in our patient interviews. In August, 1972, several patients
reported that a patient had assaulted three officers, punching one
in the face and causing a rib cage separation to another, before
he was subdued. He was then allegedly beaten up. In October,
during a pretransfer interview, a patient, when asked what he did
not like about Mid-Hudson, replied, "the brutality." He claimed
that several times he had seen an officer punch a patient who had
threatened suicide and that he had seen another officer beat up a
patient who had used a curse word in front of a nurse. Throughout the ten months that Mid-Hudson remained on the grounds of
Matteawan, there was continued conflict between the demands of
treatment and those of security. Security apparently tended
toward very harsh responses both to minor infractions and to
occasional violent outbursts by the patients.

A major contributing factor to the serious concern by the correction officers about their ability to use physical force was the frequency with which the defendants themselves were assaultive to the other patients and to the officers. Of the 210 defendants admitted during this phase of Mid-Hudson, 66 (31%) were assaultive at some time while hospitalized. Among these 66 assaultive patients, there were 119 assaults, with one patient assaulting others eight times. While the majority of these assaults were between two patients, the frequency of such violence contributed to the development of a culture of physical force among the officers. This fostered an opposition between security and treatment, when the real issue was the permissible limits of physical restraint.

One of the circumstances that contributed to Corrections-Mental Hygiene tension was the recognition by both the officers and the medical staff that not everyone in Mid-Hudson should be there. Both the Corrections and Mental Hygiene staff from time to time identified patients they felt were malingerers who should be returned to trial. From the medical perspective, they felt hamstrung because these patients were such effective actors that the courts returned them rapidly to Mid-Hudson, making the Mid-Hudson staff look bad for sending them back to court as competent. The officers felt they lived with these men for eight hours at a time and knew which patients were "doing a number" on the doctors. Because of this group, the officers seemed to go out of their way to keep things so strict that it would not become known as a place to do time where one could "beat a rap."

During this phase at Mid-Hudson, there were both pretransfer interviews of our study group and briefer interviews on other topics with all residents of Mid-Hudson. These provide more detailed information about the defendants' perspectives on Mid-Hudson than was available about the Matteawan phase. Patients were considerably more positive about the program in Mid-Hudson building in general than they were while it was in the Matteawan wards. As noted above, 40 percent of those interviewed in Matteawan said Mid-Hudson was fair or good, and none said excellent. However, among the 188 patients interviewed just prior to release from the Mid-Hudson building, 5 percent said it was excellent and 52 percent felt it was good or fair. Just as in Matteawan, there was no relationship between the seriousness of criminal charges and the level of favorableness.

This is not to say that Mid-Hudson was the place where these defendants preferred to be detained. When given the choice of Mid-Hudson or some other hospital, only 13 percent preferred Mid-Hudson. This low proportion is similar to the 14 percent of Matteawan patients who preferred to stay there rather than at another hospital. Furthermore, when 104 Mid-Hudson patients were given a hypothetical choice between remaining in Mid-Hudson or being in jail, 56 (54%) indicated that they would prefer jail to Mid-Hudson, even with its improvements over Matteawan. Again, preferences for Mid-Hudson versus other hospitals and jail were unrelated to the length of the prison sentences that the defendants faced if returned to trial and convicted. One reason for these attitudes was mentioned by one of our research staff in July, four months after the Mid-Hudson building opened.

The lack of any constructive *activity* for the patients is evident in the meaningless pacing of the floors and in the excessive amount of smoking. A number of patients expressed the opinion that jail is often more appealing, because in jail one could at least have some diversionary job or an activity to occupy the passing hours. Men who were asked to assist with our interviews [for example, interpreters or ward organizers directing the flow of patients to be interviewed] were quite willing to help even if the detail was minor—apparently any constructive activity was welcomed.

The patient responses, the ward observations, and the discussions with the correction officers and medical staff suggest clearly that there was great improvement in the quality of life in the maximum security hospital when it moved from a totally correctional setting to one which merged more directly mental health treatment ideologies with correctional custodial ideology. The tensions that developed might be expected in any facility where two conflicting ideologies attempt to coexist.

The development of the Mental Hygiene program did not stop at the move to the improved Mid-Hudson building. After ten months in this facility, the entire operation was moved about 30 miles west, to New Hampton, New York, a location still readily accessible to New York City and the upstate area. This move, plus the introduction of treatment assistants to replace the correction officers as ward staff, marked the final transformation of this maximum security facility into a Department of Mental Hygiene operation.

MENTAL HYGIENE MODEL

When the Criminal Procedure Law shifted the responsibility for the care and detention of incompetent defendants to the Department of Mental Hygiene from the Department of Correctional Services, all planning was aimed at a secure facility totally within the DMH hospital system. This facility was intended to be a short-term diagnostic and treatment unit. It was expected that most defendants would not be dangerous and could be transferred for any additional long-term treatment to existing state hospitals. Because of the state's fiscal crisis and the decreasing civil mental hospital population, Mid-Hudson was part of the wards of Matteawan State Hospital for the first six months. Running this program on a correctional model was contrary to both the spirit of the law and the goals of DMH program planners. The move to the Mid-Hudson building was an interim step to improve the prospects for treatment. DMH believed that it was essential to separate Mid-Hudson from Matteawan physically, lest the latter's 83-year record of primarily custodial detention preclude the development of an innovative treatment program. Thus, in January, 1973, after ten months in the Mid-Hudson building, the entire program was moved to New Hampton, New York, where DMH had refurbished a former youth detention facility that had a large administration building with admissions wards, three dormitory buildings with areas for recreation, dining, and visiting, and a swimming pool.

In late November, 1972, during preparations for the move to New Hampton, a major program change was made. After much negotiation with the State Department of Civil Service, a new DMH job title was developed which was designed to facilitate the replacement of the correction officers with DMH employees. The new ward staff was called Security Hospital Treatment Assistants (T.A.s). The negotiation with Civil Service involved justifying why these ward staff should be paid more than the ward attendants at the other state mental hospitals. It was demonstrated that providing a secure setting for criminally committed patients and participating in the treatment program went beyond the job requirements for other ward staff of the civil hospitals. With this shift, DMH for the first time had full control over all the staff responsible for the Mid-Hudson program. With the move to New Hampton, DMH had an entirely separate facility.

During the first eight weeks in the Mid-Hudson building with the treatment assistants, there were two major observable differences. First, the noise level on the wards greatly increased. As described by one observer during the first week, "The noise level was considerably higher than had been allowed by the correction officers and a few of the patients were playing a slapping game which eventually led to friendly punching and poking. This type of action would never have been allowed to progress to that point while the correction officers were on duty." A second observer wrote, "In general, I would say that the treatment assistants are more considerate than the correction officers were, particularly on this ward where the atmosphere had been generally one of screaming and yelling by the correction officers."

The second major change during this early period was a sharp decrease in patient reports of staff brutality. During the treatment assistants' first six weeks, not a single incident of brutality was reported. In fact, there was evidence that some patients were improving. A treatment assistant described a patient who had wet his bed every night since coming to Mid-Hudson. The patient had never talked. After two weeks with the treatment assistants, he was wetting the bed only about once a week and was talking occasionally. The treatment assistant claimed that the reason for this improvement was that the correction officers had punched this patient around a lot to get him to shape up. As a result, the patient lived in a state of constant fear. Shortly after the new ward staff appeared, the patient began to improve.

Some of the program improvements introduced by the treatment assistants were undone after the move to New Hampton, as evidenced by an incident during the week prior to the move. A patient had forced another into an homosexual act and was caught by a treatment assistant, who broke up the encounter. The next day at supper, the treatment assistant who had broken up the sexual assault called the patient a faggot, a queer, and other derisive terms in the middle of the dining hall. The patient, who was tall and heavy, retaliated by attacking the treatment assistant. When the other treatment assistants came to their colleague's assistance, one of the patient's friends, who years before had been at Matteawan with him, started swinging at the treatment assistants. The dining hall was sealed off. The treatment assistants and five other patients continued to fight, as chairs and water pitchers were thrown around. After about 30 minutes things calmed down. This ended the honeymoon between T.A.s and patients, and some of the tensions between treatment and custody perspectives that had been evident throughout Mid-Hudson's brief history reappeared.

The most immediate and obvious impact of the move to New Hampton in January, 1973, was the return to a Matteawan-style ward arrangement. Again, each ward had two major divisions, a sleeping area and a dayroom. Both the treatment assistants and the business officer for Mid-Hudson said that this separation of the sleeping area was conscious and desirable. The patients were allowed in this area only an hour and a half after lunch and after supper, in order to keep them from sleeping away the day, as they had done previously. The business officer said that two teachers had been hired for remedial reading and arithmetic, along with five occupational therapists. Also, the new space would allow for a woodworking shop and a pottery shop with a kiln and a potter's wheel.

Not surprisingly, the patients disliked the new sleeping arrangements and the loss of their privacy. Few patients liked the New Hampton facility as much as the Mid-Hudson building. Some patients who did prefer New Hampton were those who wished to escape. During the first two weeks at New Hampton, five patients escaped—an endeavor made easier, no doubt, by the less experienced security staff and by the new building, where escape routes were difficult to identify until they had been used. After one of the escapes, a patient sent a postcard with a picture of a chain gang with an empty manacle; this resulted in growing restrictions in all phases of the New Hampton operation. Several dormitory windows were bricked up, some basement windows were cinder-blocked, more counts were taken, and recreation activities were stopped for a few weeks while the walkway from the living quarters to the recreation area was covered to prevent patients from climbing over the fence.

During the first few months in New Hampton, there appeared to be an increase in harsh measures used by the ward staff in an effort to maintain the level of control they felt necessary. By the second week in New Hampton, nearly ten weeks after the treatment assistants replaced the correction officers, reports of rising staff brutality were again filtering down. One patient volunteered that it was getting "like it was at Matteawan." He claimed two staff "beat-ups" in the past week, one of which resulted in a patient's being dragged out of the mess hall. He also claimed camisoles were again being used to punish minor infractions and that he saw a treatment assistant "hitting Roger Quincy and throwing the patient on his bed for having sworn at the treatment assistant."

The following week, on the same ward, a patient claimed that the treatment assistants on one shift were slapping another patient around and, although this patient was sick, forcing him to walk. He was allegedly told that if he did not walk to the bathroom, he would get no food or cigarettes. Still another patient was supposedly placed in a camisole on this ward when he verbally objected to the treatment assistants beating up a patient. Two months later, the same types of reports were continuing to come from this ward, although not from the whole facility, as had been the case at Matteawan and the Mid-Hudson building. Patients claimed that the treatment assistants on this ward frequently locked men in seclusion rooms for incidental infractions. Patients were not permitted to go to the bathroom as punishment for noncompliance with treatment assistants' orders. We observed this type of punishment in May, 1973, when a patient was told to get away from the treatment assistants' desk. When he did not move fast enough to satisfy the treatment assistant, the patient was placed in a jacket. The treatment assistant then demanded that a second patient parade around the ward with the camisoled patient and tell everyone how good he looked in the jacket. Thus, although on a much more limited scale than before, there was still mental and physical brutality on some of the wards.

The ward staff's desire to exert strong control over the patients and the change from Matteawan to Mid-Hudson were both vividly brought out in a conversation between one of the treatment assistants and one of our research staff. After the observer had been on a ward and commented that a number of the patients he had seen were very confused and "really zonky." The treatment assistant misunderstood the limited nature of what had been intended by our observer's statement and said:

Well, you apparently knew what was going on over there.
Yeah, its called 'zonking'. We were so short of staff with two men looking over eighty men sometimes, so with patients that we knew could be trouble, when nobody was looking at medication time,

you just gave them extra stuff. You look around and a guy who is supposed to be getting 200 ccs of Thorazine a day, well you just throw an extra dose, oh 350–400 ccs a day instead of the 200 the doctor put down for him. Yeah, that would keep the guy so he wouldn't give you no problems at all. Then when Mental Hygiene came, that all changed. They took the medication away from us. We didn't give it out any more. That cut the amount of Thorazine that was used right in half.

It was fairly clear that there were still some oppressive features in segments of the Mid-Hudson program after it had become a totally DMH operation. However, some practices, such as the improper use of medication, that had been part of earlier Corrections programs had diminished. Furthermore, there was an expansion of the treatment staff of Mid-Hudson; it now included more occupational therapists, teachers, psychologists, recreational therapists, and psychiatrists. However, a strong emphasis on security, which seemingly characterizes any facility with a mandate to securely detain all its residents, remained, with restrictions on movement, sleeping, and all other activities.

Our regular visits to Mid-Hudson stopped in June, 1973, when all but a few of the 539 defendants we had interviewed had been transferred back to court, to other civil hospitals, or to the community. By this time there seemed to be a very different atmosphere in this Mental Hygiene maximum security facility than in the Correction hospital, or even in the joint DMH-Correction program in the Mid-Hudson building. These observations were supported by the formal interviews conducted with those patients being transferred and by the 57 patients in our study group who were interviewed, with all New Hampton residents, three months after the facility had opened.

The trend toward patients' becoming more favorably disposed to the facility continued. In Matteawan, 19 percent of the patients interviewed thought the place was excellent or good; 57 percent said this of the Mid-Hudson building. Of the 34 patients responding prior to their transfers from New Hampton, 73 percent (25 patients) thought the place was excellent or good. Just as with the other two interviews, there was no difference between those patients who faced the most serious criminal charges and those with lesser charges. As Mental Hygiene had greater impact on the program, the patients became more favorable. It may have become more of a place to "beat a rap."

Despite the continued increase in the number of patients favorable to Mid-Hudson, few would choose Mid-Hudson over other civil hospitals. Only 15 percent (7 of 48) of the patients interviewed said they would rather be in Mid-Hudson than in other hospitals; 13 percent of the 135 patients interviewed in the Mid-Hudson building responded in this way.

From the patient reports, it would appear that only minor changes occurred in the institution from Mid-Hudson to New Hampton and full Mental Hygiene control. Despite some overall favorable attitudes toward the Mid-Hudson facility compared to Matteawan or jail, it was not the hospital that these defendants would choose to be in. Since 82 percent had previously been hospitalized, they knew what the alternatives were within the Mental Hygiene hospital system. They preferred those to Mid-Hudson and to jail.

CONCLUSION

The conditions at the New Hampton facility, which was totally under the Department of Mental Hygiene control at the conclusion of our data collection, are for the most part typical of what now exist in New York State. Full and partial correctional models operate in other states. In all three stages of development in New York, the observations, informal discussions, and interviews within the facilities suggest conditions somewhere between the oppressive, almost completely inhumane conditions of Fredrick Wiseman's *Titicut Follies* and the open-door civil hospital so often depicted in the media. In all of the maximum security hospitals, there were severe restrictions on all types of activity, periodic physical and mental assaults, and internal tensions between treatment and security that caught the patients in the middle, often giving them the worst of both worlds.

It appears that for the majority of defendants, diversion into a maximum security mental hospital on any of these three models is not a way to "beat their raps." On the other hand, there are surely some malingerers who know the system and prefer this diversion into mental health facilities over jail. Our data suggest that this group is much smaller than has generally been thought. An estimate based on our discussions with the medical and security staffs and from our observations would be from 5 to 15 percent of the hospital's population.

The only estimate to be found in the research literature is that offered by Dr. Henry C. Weinstein, the Director of the psychiatric prison ward at Bellevue. In his review of McGarry's monograph (Weinstein 1977), he says that at least 25 percent of the patients on this ward are malingerers. He qualifies this estimate by noting that the Bellevue patients are "admittedly a selected group of difficult patients." This qualifier may explain why his estimate is slightly higher than the one we drew from our data at Mid-Hudson and Matteawan.

What malingering may have been present in our defendant group was not related to the seriousness of the criminal charges facing the defendant. There is general agreement in the research literature that incompetent defendants end up with longer detention time than defendants convicted and sentenced, so it is quite possible that many of these defendants receive legal advice along such lines. Unless incompetency was a defense tactic to facilitate a not-guilty-by-reason-of-insanity plea, mental health diversion would help little unless it positively influenced the court to fewer or less serious convictions and for shorter sentences after conviction. Chapter 6 examines whether this occurs. In any event, the data on these maximum security detention facilities show that they are not nice places to be. Limited freedom, aggressive guards and patients, homosexual assaults, and restricted treatment programs are common. For most defendants, such hospitals are restrictive and depressing.

Our data do not permit a clear delineation of the small group that has managed to get diverted through skillful acting and manipulation of medical and security staffs. What the data presented do indicate clearly is that maximum security detention facilities that now operate for incompetent defendants are not resorts that easily permit the escape of these defendants to rape and pillage the community. They may not be the snakepits of *Titicut Follies,* but they surely are not the Creedmoors of the *New York Times,* where patients regularly leave for weekend R and R.

6   Final Disposition of
Criminal Charges

What finally happens to the criminal charges faced by incompetent defendants? How many are convicted? How many end up going to prison? From the vantage points of the public and prosecutors, the ultimate questions in determining whether incompetency diversion allows defendants to "beat a rap" are the disposition of the criminal charges the defendants faced when they were found incompetent and how long the defendants were off the street compared to what would have occurred had they stayed in the prison system. This chapter answers these questions in detail. To facilitate discussion of the disposition data, we will use shorthand labels for the three defendant groups: unindicted, not-dangerous, and dangerous. The indicted defendants are included in the not-dangerous and dangerous groups.

In addition to determining the outcome of the criminal process for each of these defendants, it was important to have a yardstick with which to compare their experiences. Therefore, a study group of indicted defendants not diverted was drawn from the district attorney's records in three New York City boroughs.[1] The dispositions of these indicted felony defendants were compared with those of all defendants from our 539 defendants transferred back to court in these three boroughs during one year. This criminal justice comparison group of 88 defendants from the boroughs of Manhattan, Bronx, and Queens showed two clear differences with the incompetent defendants. First, those defendants who are processed totally within the criminal justice system after indictment are convicted at much lower rates than those defendants diverted as incompetent. Second, the incompetent defendants, although more often convicted, are less often incarcerated beyond the time served in maximum security mental hospitals.

This chapter will analyze two related sets of data. The first contains the information available on the institutional processing and final dispositions of all 539 defendants. The second includes all 88 defendants from the total study group of 539 defendants who returned to three New York City boroughs between November, 1971, and November, 1972, and a comparison group of 88 defendants selected from the indictment books of these three boroughs. The second set of data permits comparisons between the defendants diverted as incompetent and other defendants in the same jurisdictions who were not diverted.

The information on the total study group and on the comparison group strongly suggests that incompetency to stand trial is a prelude to neither a successful insanity acquittal nor a dramatically reduced period of detention in desirable facilities.

DISPOSITIONS OF THE 539 INCOMPETENT DEFENDANTS

The unindicted defendants were committed under 90-day orders. The indicted defendants were committed under one-year orders. Thus, it was not at all unexpected that the indicted defendants spent much more time in Mid-Hudson and Matteawan before they were returned to court or sent elsewhere for treatment than did the unindicted defendants. The 282 unindicted defendants spent an average of 22 weeks in Mid-Hudson before being sent elsewhere. The not-dangerous defendants sent to Mid-Hudson averaged 37 weeks there. The dangerous defendants sent to Matteawan spent an average of 46 weeks.

These differences were to be expected under the existing statutes. However, the substantial differences in where the three groups of incompetent defendants were sent after their Mid-Hudson and Matteawan detention and the ultimate dispositions of their criminal charges were not expected. Table 5 shows that most unindicted defendants were sent someplace other than court, while most indicted defendants were returned to court to stand trial. The largest proportion of the unindicted defendants, 58 percent, were sent from Mid-Hudson to regular security civil mental hospitals for further treatment. Ten percent were released directly to the community. In all 28 cases where the defendant was released directly to the community from maximum security confinement, the district attorney had indicated no interest in prosecuting the case. Only 84 of the 278 cases (30%) involving unindicted defendants were returned directly to court to stand trial.

In contrast, of the 119 not-dangerous defendants, fully 69 percent were sent from Mid-Hudson directly to court as ready to stand trial, and 60 percent of those determined to be dangerous were sent from Matteawan to court. Only 27 percent of the not-dangerous defendants and 36 percent of the dangerous defendants were sent to civil hospitals for continued treatment. As we will see below, over half of both the dangerous and not-dangerous groups sent to civil hospitals were subsequently tried. Table 5 also shows that not one of the 248 indicted defendants was discharged from Mid-Hudson or Matteawan directly to the community. At the same time, about 10 percent of the unindicted defendants were directly discharged to the community.

TABLE 5   Locations to Which Defendants Were Transferred from Maximum Security Detention

	Legal Status at Admission					
			Indicted,		Indicted,	
	Unindicted		Not Dangerous		Dangerous	
Discharge location	N	%	N	%	N	%
Civil hospital	160	57.5	32	26.9	46	35.7
Court	84	30.2	82	68.9	77	59.7
Community	28	10.1	0	—	0	—
Other	5	1.8	1	0.8	4	3.1
Not discharged	1	0.4	4	3.4	2	1.6
TOTAL*	278	100.0	119	100.0	129	100.0

* Incomplete information for 13 cases.

While there were obvious differences between the unindicted and indicted in their pathways from Mid-Hudson and Matteawan,

once in the regular security civil hospitals, there was little difference in how long they were there. The unindicted defendants
spent an average of 19 weeks before being released to the community. The not-dangerous defendants stayed about 22 weeks,
and the dangerous defendants remained about 17 weeks. Thus,
at the point of treatment in civil mental hospitals, the legal status
of these defendants made little difference in how long they remained hospitalized.

However, just as the unindicted defendants differed markedly
from the indicted defendants in where they went when transferred
from Mid-Hudson, so, too, they returned to the community in
vastly different ways. Almost all the 160 unindicted defendants
who went from Mid-Hudson to a civil hospital for further treatment were released to the community after an average of 19
weeks of confinement. In only 8 cases (5%) was the district attorney sufficiently interested in prosecuting a case to return the
defendant to be indicted after the civil hospitalization. In sharp
contrast, not only were many fewer not-dangerous defendants
sent to a civil hospital, but nearly half (15 out of 32) were sent
back to court. Similarly, only 46 dangerous defendants were
transferred to civil hospitals. Of these, 23 (50%) were eventually
sent back to court.

Among the indicted defendants who reached the community
directly from civil hospitals after transfers from Mid-Hudson and
Matteawan, 40 percent did so by escape rather than by adminis-
tratively approved discharge. Of the 17 not-dangerous defendants, 5 escaped; of the 23 dangerous defendants, 11 escaped.
The charges pending against these 16 escapees were serious,
including two for murder, two for rape, six for robbery, and one
for assault.

The fact that defendants with such serious charges, who already
had been indicted, escaped from the mental health settings might
suggest that, with these 16 defendants, we have a definable group
of defendants (3% of 539) who successfully "beat their raps."
However, even this 3 percent figure for escaping prosecution
overestimates what really happened. Of the 16 defendants who
absconded from the civil hospitals while under indictment, 7
were eventually captured and tried. Three of the 7 were acquitted.
This leaves 11 who did "beat their raps." However, this does not
mean that the defendants' prosecutions were terminated. They
reached freedom by means of the mental health system, but their

charges remain active. If they are picked up by the police, prosecution might still be attempted. Of course, the law enforcement dilemma of being unable to collect victims and witnesses two, three, or four years after a crime has occurred is well known. Thus, even should these 11 defendants be captured, they quite possibly will beat the charges they faced when they were found competent. Thus, the group of defendants who clearly "beat their raps" includes only 11 persons (2% of the total group), all escapees who were still at large at the end of our research.

From the viewpoint of the severity of the pending charges, there was little rhyme or reason for which cases were and which were not prosecuted. Of the 23 unindicted persons released directly from Mid-Hudson to the community, none involved a homicide or manslaughter charge. Of course, as noted in chapter 3, most defendants with murder charges were indicted. One community releasee case involved a rape charge, and a second case involved a sodomy charge. The most common charge was assault, which occurred in eight cases. There were seven burglary charges and two robbery charges. The other four cases were for reckless endangerment, drug possession, criminal mischief, and criminal possession of stolen property. Thus, while the majority of charges were not among the most serious, there were enough violent crimes against persons to suggest that it was not the minor nature of the charges faced by the incompetent defendants that influenced nonprosecution. Rather, it may have been the strength of the state's cases against these defendants. In the minor offenses, the maximum sentence that conviction would bring would be approximately equal to the time already spent in mental hospitals regaining competency and in jail awaiting trial. Thus, prosecution would not be worthwhile. However, the substantial number of more serious offenses included among the unindicted defendants released to the community after the district attorney had indicated no interest in prosecution would suggest that the state's case was weak. When this was considered in the context of the time already served, it was decided that justice had been served.

In addition to the defendants returned to court to stand trial after they were sent to civil hospitals for further treatment, there were 82 not-dangerous defendants and 77 dangerous defendants who went directly from Mid-Hudson or Matteawan back to court. Thus, among the two groups of indicted defendants, fully 69 percent of the not-dangerous and 60 percent of the dangerous defendants directly returned to stand trial. In sharp contrast, only 30 percent of the unindicted defendants went from Mid-Hudson directly to court. Another 3 percent went first to civil hospitals.

The drastic differences between the indicted and unindicted defendants and the use of incompetency as an easy way out for prosecutors becomes clearer when the final dispositions of the criminal charges displayed in table 6 are examined. Just over two-thirds of all unindicted cases were *not* prosecuted. By contrast, only 12 percent of the not-dangerous group and 4 percent of the dangerous group had their charges dismissed or were acquitted. On the other hand, 64 percent of the not-dangerous group and 54 percent of the dangerous group were found guilty of a felony. An additional 10 percent and 13 percent, respectively, of each group were convicted of a misdemeanor. The majority of cases that were disposed of at the end of our data collection resulted in convictions for the indicted defendants and in dismissals or acquittals for the unindicted defendants.

TABLE 6 Disposition of Criminal Charges by Legal Status on Admission

Final Disposition	Unindicted		Indicted, Not Dangerous		Indicted, Dangerous	
	N	%	N	%	N	%
Dismissed, acquitted	173	67.8	15	12.0	5	4.1
Guilty, felony	43	16.9	80	64.0	66	54.1
Guilty, misdemeanor	19	7.5	13	10.4	16	13.1
Not guilty by reason of insanity	3	1.2	4	3.2	4	3.3
Other	7	2.7	0	—	4	3.3
Pending	10	3.9	13	10.4	27	22.1
TOTAL*	255	100.0	125	100.0	122	100.0

* Incomplete information for 37 cases.

Table 6 also shows the very small number of cases among these incompetent defendants that resulted in acquittals by reason of insanity. Only 3 of the 255 unindicted cases for which information was available resulted in insanity acquittals, as did only 4 of the 83 not-dangerous cases and 4 of the 121 dangerous cases. These data directly contradict the popular conception that a primary way in which incompetency diversion helps a defendant to "beat a rap" is by providing support for successful not-guilty-by-reason-of-insanity pleas. In this large group of indicted and unindicted defendants, successful insanity pleas occurred in only 2.4 percent of all cases, about as frequently as has been estimated for the judicial process in general.

Once a defendant was convicted, there was little difference in the sentences of the indicted and unindicted defendants. Table 7 shows that 40 percent of the unindicted group were given more prison time, as were 42 percent of the not-dangerous defendants and 52 percent of the dangerous defendants. Thus, once these defendants were returned to court and were found, or pleaded, guilty, all three groups had about the same prospects of being sentenced to additional time. However, there remained tremendous differences when the entire group of defendants in each legal status was considered. The unindicted defendants included 255 whose final disposition could be determined. Of these, only 62 (24%) were eventually convicted. Of these, 24 (9% of the total group) ended up with more imprisonment as a result of the criminal charges. In contrast, of the 125 not-dangerous defendants, 93 (74%) were convicted. Thirty-seven (30%) did additional time. Similarly, of the 122 dangerous defendants for whom dispositional data were obtainable, 82 (67%) were subsequently convicted, and 40 (33%) were sentenced to further incarceration.

TABLE 7   Sentences Imposed on Cases Disposed of by Legal Status on Admission

Sentence	Unindicted N	Unindicted %	Indicted Not Dangerous N	Indicted Not Dangerous %	Indicted Dangerous N	Indicted Dangerous %
Guilty, probation	27	45.0	35	39.3	25	32.5
Guilty, incarceration	24	40.0	37	41.6	40	51.9
Guilty, time served	4	6.7	9	10.1	6	7.8
Guilty, suspended sentence	0	—	2	1.1	0	—
Guilty, conditional discharge	4	6.7	4	4.5	5	6.5
Guilty, unconditional discharge	0	—	3	3.4	1	1.3
Narcotics certification	1	1.7	0	—	0	—
TOTAL	60	100.0	89	100.0	74	100.0

It is clear that for the unindicted defendants, the maximum security mental hospitals served as a substitute for criminal conviction and incarceration. In two-thirds of such cases, indictments were never obtained, and after an average of 22 weeks in Mid-Hudson's maximum security setting and an additional 19 weeks in a regular security civil mental hospital, these defendants were returned to the community. From a purely dispositional standpoint, the state saved court and prosecution costs, while incarcerating these defendants for a period close to what they would have served if they had been convicted of their pending criminal charges. The cases handled this way involved, for the most part, less serious offenses or those for which the district attorney apparently had weak cases. Not all unindicted defendants fell into this group. Most of the remaining one-third were returned to court for indictment and criminal processing. Sixty-two (24%) were eventually convicted. However, the former course of events was by far the most typical for the unindicted defendants.

For both groups of indicted defendants, detention in the maximum security facilities was much longer than for the unindicted defendants: 37 weeks for the not-dangerous group and 46 weeks for the dangerous group. Most of these defendants, when considered no longer in need of treatment for regaining competency, were sent back to court. Most were sent directly from Mid-Hudson or Matteawan, but some returned to court after additional treatment in civil hospitals. For 21 defendants in the not-dangerous group, the average stay in the civil hospitals before returning to court was 22 weeks; for the dangerous group it was 17 weeks. However, the wait for trial did not end with transfer from a maximum security hospital to court.

The not-dangerous group waited an average of 39 weeks from the time they left Mid-Hudson to their conviction or dismissal. From the records used to gather this information, it was impossible to tell how many of the 39 weeks might have been spent in the community on bail. Given the poor economic status of most defendants and the seriousness of both the current charges and prior criminal records, most, no doubt, remained incarcerated. Thus, the 80 not-dangerous defendants who went directly from Mid-Hudson to court were detained, on the average, a total of 76 weeks after the determination of incompetency before conviction or dismissal. In addition, there was an average of 21 weeks from arrest to competency evaluation, plus 8 weeks from evaluation to admission to Mid-Hudson. Their total detention time before the dispositions of their criminal charges averaged two years (105 weeks). For the 21 defendants in the not-dangerous group who went from Mid-Hudson to a civil hospital before court, 22 weeks of predisposition detention time were added, for a total of 127 weeks. Thus, for the offenses on which many of these defendants were convicted, it made little sense to further incarcerate them for what would be an insignificant time, with the associated transportation and detention costs. For many, the maximum sentence that could have been imposed had already been exceeded.

The lengths of predisposition detention for the dangerous defendants were similar. This group spent an average of 46 weeks in Matteawan and an additional 47 weeks awaiting trial after their return to court. Added to this was 26 weeks from arrest to admission to Matteawan. They had thus been incarcerated 119 weeks, more than two years, before sentencing would have occurred. Also, 56 members of the dangerous group spent 17 weeks in civil hospitals after Matteawan and before disposition. For this group also, the minimal need for sentences imposing further incarceration is readily apparent.

When the total time spent in detention from arrest to the final disposition of the criminal charges is calculated for all 539 defendants, the possibility of prosecutors using incompetency as an easy dispositional tool becomes evident. It also becomes clear why the conviction rates, reported in table 6, are easily misinterpreted. Incompetent defendants did not need to be convicted to spend as much time off the street as if they had "copped a plea" in the usual course of the criminal process and received the usual sentence of probation or prison terms abbreviated by parole. On the average, the unindicted defendants spent 59 weeks incarcerated and the indicted groups just over two years incarcerated as incompetent or mentally ill before either returning to the community or serving further prison time after a conviction on their criminal charges.

These findings support the notion of incompetency as an easy way out of criminal prosecution and an easy way into involuntary detention for the state as much as they support it as an easy way out of a criminal sentence and an easy way to return to the community for the defendant. These 539 defendants were detained for lengthy periods in maximum security facilities without a criminal conviction. These periods were sufficiently long in comparison to the sentences for which they were liable if convicted on their criminal charges that prosecution was dropped in two-thirds of the unindicted cases. Only 47 percent of the unindicted cases resulted in additional prison time. These findings lend support to the Group for the Advancement of Psychiatry's (GAP) conclusion:

When we examine this pattern of prosecutorial use of the competency determination, it is hard to argue that the prosecutor is intentionally and maliciously exploiting his powers. Often, it seems, he is simply protecting himself and the community as he thinks in the best interest of all, but the fact is that what he does in these cases he simply could not do in ordinary criminal cases, and his additional power derives from his raising the spector of mental illness. [GAP 1974:883]

These data also contradict the previous studies that found incompetency determinations tantamount to lifelong detention. The period of detention as incompetent is quite finite. For some defendants with more serious charges, this sort of alternate disposal of the cases in the post-*Jackson* era may be preferable to conviction. Nevertheless, for most, incompetency as a dispositional ploy appears to be of more service to prosecutors than to defendants.

The data presented do not permit precise evaluation of what might have happened to these defendants had they remained in the criminal justice system and not been diverted for mental health treatment. Such an assessment is, however, crucial in answering our core question of whether incompetent defendants are "beating a rap." A more precise delineation of the impact of incompetency diversion is needed in which the experiences of diverted defendants are compared with a similar group, within the same jurisdictions, who were not diverted. With these data, a more precise determination can be made about whether, despite spending substantial time confined before disposition, incompetency still produces more rapid returns to the community. The next section of this chapter reports some information from a subsample of the 539 defendants who were compared with another group of "purely criminal" defendants who, after arrest, were not diverted from the more typical routines of the criminal justice system.

COMPARING THE DISPOSITION OF INCOMPETENT AND
CRIMINAL DEFENDANTS

To obtain meaningful comparisons between defendants diverted as incompetent and those not diverted, it was important to take defendants in both categories from the same jurisdictions. By taking the same jurisdictions, cases would be examined that were prosecuted by the same district attorneys' offices and presided over by the same judges. The choice of jurisdictions for the two defendant samples required that there be a high enough volume of cases to permit the necessary statistical analyses. As a result, we chose to examine the dispositions of all of the incompetent defendants returned to stand trial in the New York's three busiest counties, New York (Manhattan), Bronx, and Kings (Brooklyn), for one year from the date that the first defendant was returned to stand trial. This produced a sample of 88 defendants returned to stand trial between November 12, 1971, and November 11, 1972.

We wanted, so far as possible, to have in the comparison group males who were processed in these counties at the same time as the 88 incompetent defendants. This criminal comparison group was drawn by going to the indictment books maintained in each district attorney's office and locating the indictment for each of the 88 incompetent defendants. Then the indictment immediately preceding that of the incompetent defendant was selected. If this indictment was of a female or if a mental health diversion was noted, the subsequent indictment case was selected instead. This produced a group of 88 criminal defendants whose dispositions and sentences could be compared with those of the incompetent defendants. The unindicted incompetent defendants in our study group were excluded from these comparisons.

Since the criminal comparison group was chosen to control for variations in the dispositional process, it did not necessarily produce two groups with similar alleged offenses. Because the severity of the charges might be related to disposition, the first analysis of the two groups was a comparison of their indictment charges. As would be expected from the greater seriousness of the incompetent defendants' offenses compared to the general criminal offenses, the 88 incompetent defendants returned to court had charges more serious than the defendants in the comparison group. Of the 88 incompetent defendants, 26 (30%) were indicted for murder, manslaughter, assault, or rape; 43 (49%) were indicted for robbery or burglary; 12 (14%) for drugs or weapons offenses; and the remaining 7 (8%) for minor property offenses. Approximately the same number of defendants in the comparison group, 22 (25%), were charged with murder, manslaughter, assault, or rape; but substantially fewer, 21 (24%), were charged with robbery and burglary. Much more frequent among the latter group of defendants were drug and weapons offenses, which included 29 defendants (33%). More than twice as many criminal defendants as incompetent defendants were charged with minor property offenses (18%). Thus, just as the entire group of incompetent defendants faced more serious charges than would be expected based on statewide arrest rates, so, too, were those defendants indicted before being found incompetent charged with more serious offenses than those defendants indicted in the same counties but not diverted as incompetent.

Table 8 shows that the incompetent defendants were much more often convicted than the defendants in the comparison group. Whereas only 7 percent of the incompetent cases that had been disposed of at the cutoff of our data collection were dismissed or acquitted, 20 percent of the criminal group's cases were. It is clear that when a defendant is indicted and found incompetent, he almost without exception will be found guilty. Likewise, although all the defendants in both groups were indicted on felonies, there is a somewhat higher probability that the criminal defendants will be convicted on a felony (26% versus 18%). If the same defendant remains in the more usual track of criminal processing, there is a one in five chance for dismissal and a one in four chance that if convicted he will be convicted of a misdemeanor.

Because of the contrast in dismissal rates between the incompetent defendants and the criminal defendants, a second sample of incompetent defendants was taken. This second sample was added to check the possibility that many of the indicted incompetent defendants might have had their charges dismissed while they were in Mid-Hudson. If this were true, the results of our survey would have been biased in favor of a higher conviction rate among the incompetent defendants, since we would have been looking only at those defendants returned to court. Such was not the case. The disposition data on the first 72 indicted defendants admitted to Mid-Hudson were gathered. Among this group, 44 cases had been disposed of, and not one had resulted in the dismissal of charges while the defendant was in Mid-Hudson. Only one case resulted in acquittal after the defendant was returned to court. Apparently, acquittal rarely occurs among indicted incompetent defendants, while it occurs in about 20 percent of regular criminal cases.

TABLE 8   Dispositions of Indicted Incompetent Defendants and Criminal Defendant Comparison Samples

Disposition	Incompetent		Criminal	
	N	%	N	%
Guilty, misdemeanor	15	18.3	18	25.7
Guilty, felony	60	73.2	35	50.0
Dismissed, acquitted	6	7.3	14	20.0
Youthful offender	1	1.2	3	4.3
TOTAL	82	100.00	70	100.0
Pending	6		18	

$X^2 = 10.17$; $p < .02$; $C^2| = .25$

A second explanation for the discrepancies in the dispositions of the incompetent and criminal defendants centers on the fact that the incompetent defendants faced more serious criminal charges. Possibly as a result, the district attorneys were less likely to dismiss these charges and more likely to obtain convictions. Table 9 presents the dispositions of the cases within each of the four major offense categories. This table shows that, except for property offenses, the conviction rate of the incompetent defendants in each offense category is higher than for the criminal group. Although statistical significance is not obtained except for robbery and burglary, due to the small N in many cells, for most offenses, incompetent defendants were more often convicted, and more often convicted of felonies, than the criminal group. In this sense, it surely is not "beating a rap" to be diverted as incompetent.

The last stage of the criminal disposition of charges is sentencing. In comparing the sentences received by the incompetent defendants and the criminal defendants, we found that the variability of the records in the three district attorneys' offices posed some constraints. In some counties the period of probation was recorded regularly, while in others it was not. Also, the

TABLE 9 Dispositions of Incompetent and Criminal Defendants by Indictment Charge

Indictment Charge

Disposition	Murder, Manslaughter, Assault				Robbery, Burglary				Property				Drugs, Weapons, Other Criminal			
	Incomp.		Criminal		Incomp.		Criminal		Incomp.		Criminal		Incomp.		Criminal	
	N	%	N	%	N	%	N	%	N	%	N	%	N	%	N	%
Guilty, Felony	19	86.4	12	75.0	31	75.6	7	38.9	1	14.2	3	20.0	9	75.0	13	61.9
Guilty, misdem.	3	13.6	2	12.5	6	14.6	2	11.1	3	42.9	9	60.0	3	25.0	5	23.8
Dismissed, acquitted	0	—	2	12.5	3	7.3	7	38.9	3	42.9	3	20.0	0	—	2	9.5
Youthful Offender	0	—	0	—	1	2.4	2	11.1	0	—	0	—	0	—	1	4.8
TOTAL	22	100.0	16	100.0	41	99.9	18	100.0	7	100.0	15	100.0	12	100.0	21	100.0
Pending	4		6		2		3		0		1		1		8	

$X^2 = 1.81$ NS (Murder, Manslaughter, Assault)

$X^2 = 5.83$ $\rho \leq .02$ $C^2 = .30$ (Robbery, Burglary)

$X^2 = .075$ NS (Property)

$X^2 = .147$ NS (Drugs, Weapons, Other Criminal)

sentences were often missing from the indictment books. When they were given, they would state "prison, 0–indefinite." Thus, the actual sentences imposed had to be grouped rather grossly for comparison. Since our major questions involved additional detention time, we compared the sentences of the two groups, separating violent crimes from property crimes and dividing the sentences into those involving further imprisonment and those permitting immediate release to the community with or without continuing correctional supervision (see table 10).

TABLE 10   Sentences of Indicted Incompetent Defendant and Criminal Defendant Samples by Conviction Charge

	Conviction Charge							
Sentence	Actually or potentially against person				Property, drug other			
	Incompetent		Criminal		Incompetent		Criminal	
	N	%	N	%	N	%	N	%
Time served, conditional discharge, probation	16	48.5	7	33.3	16	69.6	18	62.1
Imprisonment	17	51.5	14	66.7	7	30.4	11	37.9
Total	33	100.0	21	100.0	23	100.0	29	100.0

$X^2 = .66$ NS $X^2 = .073$ NS

From these data, it appears that there is a different pattern in the violent crimes than in the property and drug crimes. Among the crimes potentially or actually against persons, there is a slight, although statistically not significant, trend for the criminal defendants, who are convicted less often than incompetent defendants, to be given prison sentences when they are convicted. Of 21 criminal defendants who were convicted of violent offenses, 14 (67%) were given prison sentences; only 17 (52%) of the incompetent defendants were given additional time. Although the differences were not as large, the same pattern existed in the property crimes. The incompetent defendants were less often given more time. The consistently less severe sentences for the incompetent defendants are not surprising. The pretrial detention time for the incompetent defendants in many instances was two years or more, so the maximum sentence they could have received when they were eventually convicted already was exceeded.

It did appear that there was a strong tendency in the courts to count the time in maximum security mental hospitals as incarceration time, although the New York State statutes did not require that such time be deducted from sentences. While the indicted incompetent defendants, almost without exception (98%), were ultimately convicted, they did their time in mental hospitals rather than prisons. Thus, whether the district attorney stopped prosecution during the hospitalization, as was typical among the unindicted, or whether prosecution ultimately resulted in a conviction, the detention time preceding trial and sentencing was seen by the court as being sufficient to substitute for imprisonment.

Because the conviction rate among the unindicted is so modest (24%), and because such a small proportion among the indicted end up with long prison sentences after their mental hospitalizations and criminal trials, the data presented in the previous chapter become even more important. In assessing what it really means to be diverted as an incompetent defendant, the conditions under which this alternate detention time is served become critical. Overall, however, the dispositions of the criminal charges of the incompetent defendants suggest as much about the use of incompetency by prosecutors to avoid prosecution of minor or weak cases as they do about misuse by defendants who are looking for a way to "beat their raps."

7   Did They Beat Their Raps?

This chapter focuses on the three major ways defendants might "beat their raps": (1) reduced length of time detained; (2) more favorable environment of confinement; and (3) increased frequency of subsequent acquittals by reason of insanity. The chapter concludes with a general discussion about the future of incompetency proceedings.

LENGTH OF CONFINEMENTS
For the general public, probably the most important issue related to "beating a rap" is how often being found incompetent allows an offender to return to the community without sufficient detention. A major contention of both the public and many professionals is that incompetent defendants return to the community much more quickly from mental hospitals than they would if they were tried and imprisoned. One aspect of this fear is the notoriety that the media and district attorneys give certain escapes by these defendants. Chapter 6 documents that escapes do happen, infrequently, even among indicted defendants. Only 5 of 114 not-dangerous defendants and 11 of 122 dangerous defendants escaped from the civil hospitals after transfer from maximum security settings. Further, of these 16 indicted escapees,

100

7 were eventually tried. These findings show that the cases of escaped mental patients with criminal charges that are periodically headlined in the media are rarities rather than commonplace.

Much more important to the question of the length of detention was the data about how long the other 93 percent of the defendants were off the street between the time they were arrested and their return to the community and how this time compared with the period they might have been locked up as a result of their pending criminal charges. The unindicted defendants, most of whom were not convicted, took an average of fifteen months to reach the street. The not-dangerous group averaged just under two years incarceration as incompetent, plus any additional time those who were convicted received. The dangerous defendants averaged two years and two months before returning to the community, plus any additional prison time. Thus, the unindicted defendants who were not given further sentences were off the streets over a year. The indicted defendants who were not given further sentences were off the streets, on the average, for about two years.

In comparing this time detained *without* criminal conviction to what they might have gotten had they not been found incompetent, there is a crucial issue that has only been mentioned in passing: plea bargaining. Plea bargaining, or "copping a plea," is the process by which a defendant agrees to plead guilty in exchange for a diminished charge. This deal permits defendants who feel they are likely to be convicted and receive fairly severe sentences, either because of the nature of the crime or because of their past records, to obtain a shorter sentence by pleading guilty to a lesser offense than the one for which they were arrested. The state is relieved of prosecuting plea-bargained cases, with the associated court costs, and, if the defendants are not out on bail, with the costs of detaining them until trial. From a political standpoint, the prosecutors can demonstrate a high conviction rate for the next election. Figures reported in the 1976 *Annual Report* of the New York State Department of Criminal Justice Services (1977) show that in the dispositions of all felony indictments in both 1975 and 1976, 92 percent of all those convicted pleaded guilty. Only 8 percent of all those convicted of a felony had a trial.

The high percentage of cases closed by plea bargains is important in evaluating the length of detentions of incompetent defendants because most of the estimates on how long they could have been detained had they not been diverted are calculated either from charges made at the time of their arrests or from indictment charges. While such charges may be important in reflecting the illegal behavior that they allegedly engaged in, using these charges radically overestimates how long defendants would have been detained within the criminal justice system. It is an overestimate because if the defendants had continued through the court system, nine out of ten cases that resulted in convictions would have involved pleas of guilty in return for diminished charges. Thus, the defendant charged with Robbery, First Degree, maximum sentence 25 years, might plead guilty to Robbery, Third Degree, maximum sentence 7 years. The same holds true for rape, assault, burglary, larceny, or whatever: how long a defendant is liable to be incarcerated is substantially less than what is indicated by the arrest or indictment charge.

Furthermore, when an offense such as Rape, Second Degree, with its maximum sentence of 7 years, is reduced to Sexual Abuse, with its four-year maximum sentence, even the 4-year maximum sentence is not imposed in many cases. What started out at the time of arrest as an offense that could result in the defendant's spending 7 years in prison reduces to one with a maximum of only 4 years. When this reduced maximum sentence is compared to the sentence actually imposed, it becomes evident that if the time spent in jail awaiting trial is counted against this sentence, as it must be, the plea bargain in effect means that there is no need to impose additional incarceration time. For example, let us take an incompetent defendant who faces a charge of Manslaughter, First Degree. If he is the average not-dangerous indicted defendant, he will spend about 7 months in jail prior to his psychiatric evaluation; if he is found incompetent, he will spend 9 more months in Mid-Hudson; and if then returned as competent, 10 months in jail awaiting trial. If, at this time, he pleads guilty to Criminally Negligent Homicide and receives a maximum sentence of 4 years, almost all of this time will have been served. Of course, only the time spent in jails has to be counted in the sentence. However, the courts seem to count all time detained in hospitals for incompetency.

Even further diminishing how long a defendant is detained within the criminal justice system is the accumulation of "good time." In New York State, this means that one-third of the maximum sentence is subtracted upon conviction if the offender does not violate prison rules. Thus, his total prison time is two-thirds of his already reduced sentence. As a result, few offenders actually spend the full time to which they are sentenced. Their imprisonments are doubly reduced from what appears to be facing them at the time of arrest or indictment. Yet it is these artificial maximum sentences against which the detention times of the incompetent defendants are typically compared. This is tremendously misleading because such comparisons do not consider the plea bargain, the actual sentence imposed, and the release on parole after a third or a half of the imposed sentence is served.

Consider the following hypothetical newspaper account. "Sam Jones, an ex-mental patient was arrested today for breaking and entering. He had been arrested 18 months ago for breaking into another home while its residents were asleep. At that time he was found incompetent to stand trial and had been released from Central Hospital after 13 months." This account does not consider, with its implications of a very rapid return to the community after arrest, that had Sam Jones been convicted of his prior offense, he probably would have been back on the street as quickly or even more quickly. With a plea bargain, he could have been put on probation and released immediately. Indeed, he could have been on bail while the plea bargain was struck. Even if he had remained in custody or had been given a prison sentence, he could easily have been back on the street within two years. Because "Sam Jones" returned to the street after detention in a mental hospital, the media compared the maximum sentence that he could have received for the offense on which he was arrested and assumed that he would have been imprisoned for nearly that maximum sentence had he not found his way to a mental hospital. Such is not the case. From a law enforcement standpoint, neither the typical criminal justice process nor the mental health diversion is desirable. The length of incapacitation is simply not seen as sufficient in either instance. Nevertheless, it is crucial in weighing the question of the relative detention time of the incompetent defendants to compare their experiences with a realistic picture of what actually happens to those defendants who remain in the more common pathways of the court process.

Overall, for most incompetent defendants, particularly those who are not indicted, mental hospitals are simply an alternate place to do time. This is particularly true for the unindicted defendants because so few are subsequently convicted. Just over half of the indicted defendants are eventually convicted. Many do get and serve additional prison time, but many others are given "time-served" sentences in recognition of the length of time they were hospitalized. The detention times of these incompetent defendants make a much stronger case for the use of this diversion as an easy way for the state to detain defendants in very secure facilities without the ordeal of prosecution. However, it is quite clear that the GAP conclusion that "the finding of incompetency may well result in the worst possible outcome for the defendant— a lifetime sentence to a hospital for the criminally insane" (GAP 1974:889) is no longer accurate in the post-*Jackson* era. Certainly, in answer to the first major question about "beating a rap," it appears that the length of time most of these defendants are off the street is quite similar to what would have resulted had they remained in jail.

MAXIMUM SECURITY DETENTION

Because it appears that most incompetent defendants do their detention time in mental hospitals, the day-to-day existence in these facilities is critically important in answering questions about "beating a rap." If these facilities are open-door hospitals, permitting easy escape and offering programs that barely restrict human freedoms, they would clearly be preferable to a state prison system or to county jails. This would provide strong support to arguments that incompetency permits defendants to "beat their raps."

As chapter 5 showed, the New York hospitals to which these defendants were sent were maximum security institutions that seriously restricted the defendants' freedoms. Whether it was Matteawan, a mental hospital in the traditional correctional mold of minimum program and maximum security, or the evolving Mental Hygiene maximum security hospital, Mid-Hudson, very few of the defendants preferred these hospitals to the other hospitals in the state system, where treatment was geared to an open-door policy. The two times the Mid-Hudson patients were asked which they preferred, 85 percent and 87 percent, respectively, said they preferred other hospitals, and 80 percent of the Matteawan defendants preferred other hospitals.

These preferences do not mean that these patients preferred jail to hospitalization. Surprisingly, only one-third of the Matteawan patients, when given the hypothetical choice, said they would prefer to be in jail. It appeared that the Matteawan preferences were related to the seriousness of the defendants' charges, which carried with them a higher certainty of conviction and further imprisonment. Since many of the defendants in both Matteawan and Mid-Hudson were unsure how their mental hospitalization would influence the courts, it seemed that the Mid-Hudson patients were more anxious to get back into the criminal justice system to have their charges disposed of. After disposition, they assumed they would return to the community more rapidly than they would if they remained in mental hospitals for what appeared to them to be indefinite periods.

What both the Mid-Hudson and Matteawan patients did prefer was other civil mental hospitals. Unfortunately for them, the Department of Mental Hygiene, with the new responsibilities given it for the treatment of incompetent defendants by the 1971 CPL, developed a maximum security mental hospital. Previously, such detention occurred either in maximum security correctional mental hospitals or regular civil mental hospitals. In the correction model, lifelong commitments were not uncommon; in the civil model escapes were not uncommon.

Where states develop maximum security treatment programs within a mental health model, the circumstances and implications of incompetency diversion may be considerably different from either the correctional or civil ends of the spectrum. Under a maximum security mental health arrangement, the defendant is not free to roam around the institution indiscriminately and walk out. Neither is the defendant shunted to the back wards and put on high doses of tranquilizing medication. Instead, secure retention is usually assured and varying amounts of treatment may be provided. The limits that are placed on the development of a treatment program in any facility with a dual mandate of detention and treatment have been discussed by us elsewhere (Steadman, Cocozza, and Lee, 1978). Suffice it to note here that increasingly humane treatment for incompetent defendants can be developed. However, as long as these facilities are required to keep the defendants securely as well as to treat them, any mental health treatment program will be severely compromised.

Just how good a deal incompetency is for defendants depends

heavily on which of the three models discussed in chapter 5 is operating. Under the Corrections model, there is little apparent difference between mental hospitals and prisons. As Morris (1968) has noted, the defendant may, in fact, receive the worst of the correctional and mental health worlds. Certainly, our observations and interviews in Matteawan and Mid-Hudson during their earliest phases showed a lack of rehabilitation programs, wide restrictions on basic freedoms, and inhumane treatment of patients. The setting could hardly be characterized as therapeutic.

As the influence of a mental health model became more dominant in the program, as was evidenced by the addition of more psychiatrists and other mental health professionals, and the replacement of the correction officers with therapy aides, the patients scored lower on questions measuring prisonization, indicating less custodial attitudes toward the institution, and our observations suggested that the facility was an improved place for incompetent defendants to be. In those states where there may be a centralized facility under Mental Health auspices or some mixed Correction/Mental Health model, there is more apt to be a humane environment, although severe restrictions on the defendant remain. Such hospitals are not the Bridgewater State Hospital of *Titicut Follies* infamy, nor are they the open-door state hospitals decried in the *New York Times*. They fall somewhere in between.

Regardless of where these facilities for treating the incompetent defendants fall on the spectrum of corrections vs. mental health, they are not a good place to do time. Just how oppressive they are varies by state and by facility. However, under few conditions are they as open as the public may think or as beneficent as some judges claim. They are alternate places to do time that in many cases are practically the same as prisons. The major differences would be found in those states where incompetency detention is in a regular state mental hospital rather than in a maximum security facility such as those studied in New York.

Acquittals by Reason of Insanity

On our research team's first trip to one of the competency evaluation locations in New York City, the director of the institution described its intake procedures. He said that about half of the defendants who were referred for evaluation were rejected for admission after a 15- to 30-minute preliminary screening interview. He said that the medical staff was concerned that they not admit large numbers of defendants who were obviously competent, partly because many lawyers who were planning to enter a plea of not guilty by reason of insanity (NGRI) tried to have their clients admitted for competency evaluations. He said the lawyers felt that if they could show that there was sufficient question about the mental ability of their clients to proceed with a trial, they had one leg up on a successful insanity defense.

These observations by a skilled psychiatrist with much experience in forensic psychiatry, along with the increasing public awareness of the insanity questions precipitated by the "Son of Sam" case, led us to expect that there might be many cases among those of the incompetent defendants we studied that would ultimately be disposed of as NGRI. Contrary to our expectations, those of many other authors, and of the media, in only 11 of the 502 cases (2%) that had been disposed of were the defendants found not guilty by reason of insanity. Interestingly, this 2% figure exactly matches that given by Morris (1968) for insanity pleas in all cases that reach trial. Based on the exceedingly small number of cases in which NGRI acquittals did occur, we can say confidently that the NGRI defense is not a typical way for incompetent defendants to avoid prosecution and prison, and "beat a rap."

In sum, considering the length of time the incompetent defendant is actually off the street, how this time compares with what might have been given to him by the courts, the hospitals in which incompetent defendants serve time, and the infrequency of NGRI acquittals, very few incompetent defendants can be seen as "beating their raps." However, some do. Who these defendants are, and how many there are, is our next issue.

THE MALINGERERS

Those defendants who the medical and security staff feel are trying to "beat their raps" are termed malingerers. These are the people the staff think are "faking it" so they can get a better deal for themselves. The malingerers are seen as not having any "real" symptomatology, but because of their ability to fake mental illness, they convince judges or attorneys that they are incompetent. Such was the case discussed in chapter 5, where a psychiatrist said a particular defendant was competent and should be sent back to court. However the psychiatrist was certain that the defendant would "fake it" so convincingly if he were sent back, that the judge would return him directly to Mid-Hudson, an action that would reflect badly on the facility. Therefore, the defendant was allowed to stay in Mid-Hudson.

Just how many malingerers there are was one of the most difficult things to determine from this research. Based on comments from the correction officers on the wards of Mid-Hudson and Matteawan and on discussions with the staff psychiatrists, we estimated that the number was somewhere between 5 and 15 percent. The only estimate of malingerers found in the research literature was a 25 percent figure given for the psychiatric prison ward at Bellevue by its director (Weinstein 1977). This Bellevue group was thought to be a particularly difficult one, which suggested that statewide the proportion of malingerers would be lower, perhaps within our estimates for all of Mid-Hudson.

On more concrete indicators, such as conviction and incarceration rates after return to court, it appeared that the number of defendants who actually do "beat their raps" by getting more quickly to the street was possibly even lower than the estimated number of malingerers. Since the conviction rate of the incompetent defendants was higher than for "purely criminal" defendants, and because all classes of incompetent defendants were detained for so long before release or final disposition, there was no particular advantage in being found incompetent so far as returning more quickly to the street was concerned. The one group that was clearly ahead of the game included the indicted defendants who, after leaving Mid-Hudson or Matteawan, were transferred to regular security civil hospitals, escaped, and were not prosecuted. This subgroup included only 11 defendants, or 2 percent of the 539 defendants followed.

Some impressionistic data from Mid-Hudson interviews and records suggested the possibility of a network of malingerers using incompetency to "beat a rap." This possibility was suggested by the numbers of brothers and friends from the same neighborhoods who were part of the study group. On the basis of simple probabilities, there would be little chance that among 539 defendants you would find two sets of brothers, one set of stepbrothers, one set of cousins, and nine respondents who in their pretransfer interviews indicated that many of their friends in the community had been in Matteawan themselves or knew people who had been. Yet these sets of relationships were found among our study group. Given the number of prior arrests and convictions among the defendants in this study, it seems probable that there was something of an underlying criminal subculture that functioned as an information system. Many of these defendants met on prior incarcerations or hospitalizations. Nevertheless, the number of relatives and friends among these incompetent defendants suggest either that there is a tremendously strong genetic and environmental contribution to incompetency or that the word was around that Mid-Hudson and Matteawan were good places to do time. The information we have about this is impressionistic but intriguing.

Frank Greenly and Larry Franklin grew up within a couple of blocks of each other. Neal Roach said a few of his friends had brothers who had been in Matteawan, so he knew about the place. Ronald McFee said some of the guys he hung around with in New York City had been in Matteawan. Fred Grant said, "pretty much everyone has been here from the street." Willie Tyler said he knew about Mid-Hudson before he got there because a very good friend on the street had been there. During the community follow-up pilot work, we located John Simpson in Bedford-Stuyvesant and, after chatting with him for a few minutes, he asked us if we would like to go to Sam Woodward's house right around the corner. Sam had also been in Mid-Hudson. David and Clay Thompson were brothers, as were John and Charles Cappi. Jose Legron and Raphael Gonzalez were step-brothers. Nelson Keyes and Carlos Candelario were cousins.

As these friendship and family networks became apparent, there was some suggestion that one of three things was happening: (1) the mental illness associated with incompetency had strong genetic and environmental influences that linked incompetency to certain families and neighborhoods; (2) the word was out that Matteawan and Mid-Hudson (which in the minds of most of these defendants were the same place) were good places to go; or (3) the availability of this mental health diversion as an option that could be used was more apparent to these defendants who had been through the courts many times and knew one another than to persons less experienced with jails and courts. Unfortunately, our data do not suffice to distinguish adequately which of these three explanations is the most accurate. It seems unlikely that an epidemiological answer linking genes and the stresses of certain neighborhoods would hold up under testing. If we were talking only about classic cases of schizophrenia, a genetic-environmental explanation would be a more viable possibility, given recent research findings. However, the mental diseases associated with incompetency did not appear to fit such a classical picture. Either of the other two explanations is more likely. So far as preferring Matteawan as an option, some defendants expressed very strong opinions about the stigma attached to such institutions. Don Stanley, in his pretransfer interview, said that he did not plan to tell anyone he had been in a mental hospital because "old friends might expect that I was in jail if they didn't see me for a while. It was no big thing. It was almost acceptable, but if they knew I was in a mental hospital, they'd think something was wrong with me."

In sum, there are strong indications from four years of data collection that there is a small group of defendants who are familiar with the use of incompetency as a way to "beat their raps," but this group certainly is less than 15 percent of all such defendants. For many defendants, in fact, a mental hospital of any type is among the most undesirable locations to which they could be sent. Unfortunately, our data cannot more definitely identify the few malingerers.

THE FUTURE OF INCOMPETENCY
To assess the direction that the use of incompetency might take in the United States' criminal justice and mental health systems in the near future, there are three major questions that can be productively examined: (1) Since the *Jackson* decision, is incompetency getting to be a better deal for defendants? (2) Exactly what do defendants need to be competent to do? and (3) Will legal professionals actually be required to see the facilities to which defendants are committed so that they can make more informed judgements?

Is Incompetency Getting to Be a Better Deal?
The information we have presented here from a large group of incompetent defendants suggests such defendants are no longer acutely exposed to the dangers of lifelong commitment after

being found incompetent. This study is the first comprehensive follow-up of incompetent defendants since the important *Jackson v. Indiana* decision in 1972, requiring that a defendant who is not expected to regain competency within a reasonable period of time cannot be detained for treatment under criminal orders of detention. If the state thinks that such an individual requires long-term psychiatric treatment, application for retention must be made under civil statutes for involuntary detention. Such statutes are usually more stringent than incompetency statutes because higher standards of proof are required to demonstrate a person's dangerousness or impaired judgment for commitment and there are less restrictive criteria for release.

With the *Jackson* decision came guidelines that, if enforced, would effectively eliminate the type of situation that McGarry and his colleagues found rampant in Bridgewater State Hospital in the late 1960s, where many defendants with relatively minor charges were spending 15 to 20 years in Bridgewater. Informed reviews showed they were clearly capable of standing trial and probably had been for many years. Influenced by these findings, similar cases in our work on the Baxstrom patients, and the work of several of other researchers (Rubin 1972; Thornberry and Jacoby 1976), serious questions were posed about the benefit a defense attorney was providing to his client by raising the issue of incompetency. In many cases, the results were excessively long confinements in hospitals for the criminally insane that were demonstrably oppressive and inhumane. Court decisions dealing with Dannemora and Matteawan State Hospitals in New York, Farview State Hospital in Pennsylvania, and Lima State Hospital in Ohio, among others, have stated the judicial view that these hospitals have not been treatment facilities, but have provided only a particularly heinous type of involuntary detention for individuals not convicted of any crime.

From the experiences of the 539 defendants we studied, it is clear that changes have been made. New York and many other states are shifting responsibilities for the care of incompetent defendants from corrections departments to departments of mental health on the assumption that such detention will be more humane and therapeutic. This can be no more than an assumption until state mental hospitals demonstrate the ability to provide efficacious treatment programs. However, even in those locales where the state mental hospitals have few programs, it is easier to demonstrate that the retention of incompetent defendants placed in mental health department facilities is contingent upon some right to treatment and that they have the same rights and protections available to all civilly committed patients. In the past, incompetent defendants were often given neither the protection of civil commitment criteria nor the due process protection that they would have been entitled to within the criminal justice system. With current developments under the *Jackson* guidelines, their detentions are more closely allied to the criteria for involuntary mental patients, and incompetent defendants are obtaining greater due process protection.

A second major change in the post-*Jackson* era that was reflected in our data was a determination of what might be considered a "reasonable period of time" within which the defendants could be expected to become competent under the language of *Jackson*. Such a period roughly approximates the time that they would have been detained in the criminal justice system had they not been diverted. The maximum security mental hospitals studied were mainly alternate places to do time. If these facilities do change, as they have in New York State, from the purely correctional to the mental health model, and if they continue to improve, they may become better places to do time than state prisons or county jails. If this occurs, incompetency might become a much better deal and a more frequent defense tactic.

The impression developed during our research was that many of the ward staff, even after the total changeover to Mental Hygiene, did their best to prevent such a change. Because they were convinced that they could identify the malingerers who had "snowed" the doctors, and because they did not want more of these types on the wards, they made sure that life for those defendants was not any easier than it had to be under the hospital's regulations. Despite this, it does seem that in New York, at least in the years immediately after the *Jackson* decision, incompetency to stand trial did become a better deal. However, it still is not the deal that the district attorneys, judges, and the media make it out to be.

Competent for What?

It was noted in chapter 2 that fitness to proceed with trial included such things as ability to understand the criminal charges, to understand the court processes, and to cooperate with an attorney in building a defense. Surely, any judicial proceeding is sufficiently complicated that most laymen need professional guidance to participate and know what is going on. Actually, a defendant who has been arrested many times is often much more informed about court processes than most other Americans. Nevertheless, the U.S. courts, as spelled out in *Pate* v. *Robinson* (383 U.S. 375, [1966]), require that any defendant who in the eyes of the court might not meet the common law standards for standing trial be evaluated for competency. Reflection about the dispositions of these defendants, especially the comparison group of "purely criminal" defendants, poses the question, Competency for what?

Examination of the convictions of all indicted felons in New York in 1975 and 1976 showed that 92 percent of these convictions occurred by means of a guilty plea. In these cases, competency meant the ability of a defendant to understand the possible outcomes of a trial and, with the advice of a lawyer, to decide whether it would be advantageous to plead guilty to a lesser offense. The lawyer usually knows the judge who will try the case, and he is aware of probable sentences. Also, the lawyer usually consults with an assistant district attorney to get some idea about the state's interest in prosecuting on the maximum charge and about the strength of the state's case. The lawyer then presents this information to the defendant, usually with a recommendation about the best course of action. The client must decide whether to stand trial and hope for a not-guilty verdict, knowing that if he is convicted, it may be on the charge as stated and may mean a sentence far in excess of what could have been worked out in a plea bargain. Thus, the level of mental functioning required centers on making an informed choice between pleading guilty to a lesser offense versus going to trial. Surely such a decision is complicated, even if it does require somewhat less comprehension and participation than would a court trial. However, current procedures make no allowance for the realities of the criminal justice system's policies of plea bargaining, and what may be a lower level of competency required to understand them. In New York, almost all defendants see the plea bargain as the desirable course of action.

It seems that the test of adequate mental condition centers on whether the defendant can understand the deal a lawyer has set up for him and whether it is a good enough deal to justify a guilty plea. Since, in many cases, the defendant has committed the crime that he is charged with, the question becomes whether a convincing enough case can be developed for the jury to acquit him. Clearly, that is not possible in many instances, so the defendant's choice is often not a complicated one—he would be foolish not to "cop a plea." As yet, there has been little statutory recognition of the possibility of a revision of the standards for competency determinations that would acknowledge what actually occurs in the criminal justice system rather than what exists in theory. As Slovenko noted:

> The practical question is really not whether the accused is able to undergo trial, but rather whether or not he is fit to plead. It is common knowledge that, in the vast majority of cases, there is no trial. A criminal trial is in fact a rarity. . . Theoretically, in plea bargaining or in the acceptance of a guilty plea, the plea must be entered voluntarily, with an understanding of the charge and consequences of the plea; and the judge must satisfy himself that a factual basis exists for the plea. But since the proceeding is clandestine, it might be suggested that only incompetency to plead ought not to be waivable. Accordingly, a number of courts have recently stated that the standard for competency to plead guilty is more exacting than the triability standard. [1977:187]

Will Judges, D.A.s, and Attorneys Ever See These Facilities?
We observed 175 competency hearings over a one-year period and were amazed at the "wisdom" dispensed by the lawyers, judges, and psychiatrists during the course of the hearings about the institutions to which the defendants were often sent. Of about 35 judges, 12 attorneys, 6 district attorneys, and 12 psychiatrists, not one had ever seen or been inside either of the two facilities to which the incompetent defendants were committed. Despite this, it was not unusual to hear judges talk of how much good it would do a defendant to get away from the city for a while and get some attention at the Matteawan "campus," or to hear a psychiatrist talk about the improvement that might be expected within six months if a defendant were found incompetent and sent to Mid-Hudson; or to hear a district attorney complain that all the defendants who were sent to Mental Hygiene facilities escaped and would never face their criminal charges.

There might be more appropriate administration of justice in competency determinations if the decisionmakers were required to see the facilities to which they commit defendants. The psychiatrists and the attorneys get some feedback from defendants who spend time in such hospitals and either return after regaining competency or recirculate through the system after another arrest. The judges also see some of these defendants over and over again. Nevertheless, it is hard to understand the sweeping statements about what will be good or bad for these defendants made by professionals who do not have any firsthand information about the facilities to which their decisions remand these defendants. Few of these same professionals would send their children to schools, physicians, dentists, or the like, without first looking at the campus or the office. Such logic, however, is not extended to their decisions about the living arrangements to which they daily commit incompetent defendants.

What About Society's Rights?

This chapter has concentrated on the rights of the defendants and the uses of incompetency determinations as convenient devices for either the defense or the prosecution in a criminal trial. Obviously there is another important question about the rights of the community to be protected from repetitive and sometimes violent individuals who are certified by the courts as having a mental defect. We have talked about whether competency is becoming a better deal for the defendant. What about for society?

The most important thing to recognize in answering this question is that the treatment that incompetent defendants receive when committed is not primarily concerned with what they might do when they return to the community. The sole statutory purpose of incompetency diversion is to provide treatment for these defendants in order that they may become capable to stand trial. The state is not providing psychiatric treatment in order to reduce recidivism among incompetent defendants. In the public's mind, the psychiatric treatment given to alleged or actual criminals is geared to reduce the violence they might cause after their release. This is an issue misunderstood both by the public and by many criminal justice and psychiatric professionals.

Psychiatrists treat mental illness among criminals in order to reduce the symptoms associated with the malady. It is quite possible that the successful treatment of such symptoms may make the offender a more effective and active criminal. For example, consider a person who is tremendously depressed and barely functioning, and who is arrested and convicted for stealing some food that he could not afford after he got fired from his job as a stockboy. Hypothetically, after receiving psychiatric treatment while incarcerated, he might become reemployed and begin stealing larger items or embezzling. Because of his improved mental condition, he could now be much more effective at his illegal activities. In this hypothetical case, the psychiatric treatment would be measured as successful, even though recidivism increased. Thus, society's sole right is that a person charged with a crime be detained until he is able to stand trial. It was clear from the data presented on the 539 incompetent defendants that society's rights in this regard are very rarely abridged.

This hypothetical case also illustrates some of the discrepancies between widespread expectations of psychiatric treatment of offenders, incompetent and otherwise, and what realistically should be expected to be delivered. In any group of defendants receiving such treatment, a logical question is What happened to them after they got out of mental hospitals and jails? Were many of them arrested? Were they charged with violent crimes? How well did they function? Such questions are not central to the questions of whether these defendants were able to "beat a rap," but they are intriguing queries that our epilogue probes. It should be remembered that what is most important in relationship to how incompetency diversion affected criminal charges is data about where the defendants did their time and how long they were off the street. Questions about what happened to them after they got out are relevant to some of the diversion issues discussed in chapter 1 because diversion programs are intended to be more humane alternatives and to lead to greater rehabilitation. However, questions about subsequent community behavior should not be seen as core questions about whether these defendants "beat a rap" because a lower recidivism rate was not the goal of the treatment they received as incompetent defendants. Nevertheless, data about this subsequent behavior is useful in completing our picture of the defendants diverted as incompetent to stand trial.

Epilogue—Back in the Community

This chapter will examine what happened to the incompetent defendants after they returned to the community. Some defendants returned to the community directly from Mid-Hudson; others went from Mid-Hudson and Matteawan to civil hospitals and from there to the community; another large group returned to stand trial and were acquitted, sentenced to time served, or received probation—all of which put them back on the street; and finally, some defendants returned to trial, were given additional prison time, and were released after serving some portion of their maximum sentences. Not all of the 539 defendants returned to the community between September 1, 1971, and June 30, 1974. Some remained hospitalized until the end of the research, and some remained incarcerated beyond the cutoff date. We will examine what happened to the 411 defendants who returned to the community during the follow-up.

The discussion focuses primarily on the subsequent criminal activity of these defendants and secondarily on their rehospitalization experiences. Information on recidivism and rehospitalization was obtained for the entire study group. It provides a comprehensive statistical view of a group of individuals who had been arrested often before being found incompetent, and who were often arrested after their return to the community. Just as most of their prior criminal activity was for nonviolent crimes, so, too, was most of their subsequent criminal activity.

We also studied how well the group who returned to the community functioned. This aspect of our follow-up looked at mental and social functioning as well as at arrests and rehospitalization rates. A small-scale follow-up was undertaken of the first 79 patients released to the community in New York City. Our intention was to locate as many of these individuals as possible and to ascertain what they thought psychiatric treatment had done for them and how they were feeling now. This information was obtained by interviewing them during the first, third, and sixth months they were in the community. A large portion of the 79 persons we attempted to locate were reinstitutionalized before they could be found, and we encountered many difficulties in finding these persons, who were marginal in every sense of that term. As a result, we were able to interview only 27 former defendants. The data obtained from these interviews offer an interesting supplement to the large-scale statistical picture of all the defendants who returned to the community. It was apparent from the interviews that even those former defendants who had stayed out of trouble were not functioning very well. Many had been in much better condition when they were interviewed prior to their discharge from Mid-Hudson. We will first look at the total group of defendants who returned to the community during the research period, then turn to the follow-up information.

Overview of Community Behavior

Recidivism

Of the 539 defendants, 411 returned to the community and, therefore, were at risk of rearrest and rehospitalization during our follow-up. The average length of time they had been in the community following their release was approximately 18 months. Of the group at risk of rearrest, 182 (44%) were arrested at least once. Ninety-nine defendants were arrested once, 33 were arrested twice, and 50 were arrested three or more times. There were no statistically significant differences in the recidivism rates between indicted and unindicted defendants, although the unindicted defendants were rearrested somewhat less often (40% compared to 52%).

The rates of rearrest among these defendants are comparable to the rates reported in various studies of prison inmates. Daniel Glaser (1969) points out that the frequently cited figure of two-thirds of released inmates recidivating probably does not reflect all inmates released, but refers to certain facilities that house repeated offenders. Thirteen studies reviewed by Glaser included parolees who may have been returned for such technical violations as associating with known criminals or leaving their states of residence, so the actual number of ex-inmates rearrested for new criminal offenses is probably lower than these figures indicate. A recent study with North Carolina inmates found a recidivism rate over four years to be identical with that for our incompetent defendants, 44 percent. While a vast amount of other data might be referred to, it is sufficient for our purposes to note the close similarity between the rates of rearrest among these incompetent defendants and released inmates in many other studies. These similarities are critical because of the vast discrepancy between this 44 percent recidivism rate and those of mental patients generally. This discrepancy strongly suggests that among these incompetent defendants recidivism is much more linked to criminality than to mental illness.

In a study we recently completed on a sample of all patients released from New York State mental hospitals in fiscal 1975 (Steadman et al. 1978) it was determined that only 9 percent of all released mental patients were arrested over a year and a half. This converts into an annual arrest rate of 98 per 1,000 released mental patients. This rate is three times that of the general population's 32 per 1,000. However, just as with the incompetent defendants, there are vast differences in the arrest rates of those mental patients with prior police records and those without them. For instance, those released patients with no arrests prior to hospitalization have an arrest rate of 22 per 1,000, which is much lower than the general population's 32 per 1,000. Those patients with one prior arrest were rearrested at a rate of 138 per 1,000; and those with two or more previous arrests, at a rate of 414 per 1,000. Thus, within the mental patient population there is an identifiable group who are arrested much more often than most patients. This is the group that has had many prior contacts with the police.

The same is true among the incompetent defendants. While incompetent defendants are arrested much more often than other ex-mental patients, this is explained by the large number of defendants with lengthy prior criminal records, an average of 3.4 arrests per defendant. In any group with this high a level of prior criminal activity, an overall recidivism rate of 44 percent or more would not be unexpected.

While a very substantial portion of all three incompetent defendant groups were rearrested, most of the arrests were not for crimes against persons. Fully 88 percent of those released were *not* arrested for murder, manslaughter, or assault. Just as with total arrests, there was no statistically significant relationship between the defendant's legal status and type of subsequent arrest. Among the unindicted defendants, 89 percent had no subsequent arrests for violent crimes; 88 percent of the not-dangerous group and 83 percent of the dangerous defendants had no such arrests. A relatively small number of defendants in all three groups became involved in violent crimes after release. There were very few arrests after release for rape or other sex crimes. Of the 411 released defendants, only 11 (3%) were subsequently rearrested for sex crimes.

Which defendants were rearrested? Could they have been picked out ahead of time? In some ways, yes. Basically, the rearrested were those defendants who were the most often arrested before they were found incompetent. They were also younger. Table 11 shows how strong is this association between prior and subsequent arrests. Among those defendants who had no arrests prior to the one for which they were found incompetent, 22 percent were arrested after their release. However, the percentage arrested systematically increases as the number of prior arrests increases. Thirty-nine percent of those with one arrest were re-arrested. The percentage continues to increase until we reach those with 9 or more prior arrests, 77 percent of whom were rearrested. A prior record of arrests had by far the strongest relationship of all the factors related to rearrest.

Age was a second factor in our study that was consistently related to recidivism, as it has been in almost all studies of criminal recidivism. The main age distinction is between those individuals under 40 years of age and those over 40. Among the defendants under 40, 47 percent were arrested, compared to 31 percent of the released defendants over 40. Up until age 40, there were no substantial differences in the age groupings, with just

TABLE 11   Total Subsequent Arrests by Total Prior Arrests for Incompetent
            Defendants Released to the Community

Total subsequent arrests	Total prior arrests									
	0		1		2		3-9		9 or more	
	N	%	N	%	N	%	N	%	N	%
0	82	78.1	33	61.1	24	53.3	75	52.4	15	23.4
1	17	16.2	15	27.8	14	31.1	32	22.4	21	32.8
2	3	2.9	1	1.9	3	6.7	17	11.9	9	14.1
3 or more	3	2.9	5	9.3	4	8.9	19	13.3	19	29.7
TOTAL	105	100.0	54	100.0	45	100.0	143	100.0	64	100.0

$X^2 = 64.41$; $p < .001$; $C^2 = .368$

under half of each group rearrested.[1] However, regardless of age, the most important factor in identifying those defendants who were rearrested was the length of their previous criminal careers.

Among the 411 defendants who returned to the community, only two were known by the general public. The first attained notoriety by being convicted of murdering a teenage woman in Queens after his release. The second achieved dubious fame by allegedly murdering a psychologist who had treated him before his escape from Manhattan State Hospital. The first person, Joseph Baldi, had been admitted to Mid-Hudson in October, 1971, charged with, but not indicted for, the attempted murder of a police officer in Queens. He was discharged as improved in November, 1971, and was transferred to Creedmoor Psychiatric Center in Queens, from which he was released on convalescent care in January, 1972. After terrorizing the borough of Queens for three months, Baldi was arrested on June 22, 1972, for the murder of a 15-year-old girl in Jamaica. The *New York Daily News* headlined the arrest with "Seize Psycho as Sex Stabber." The newspaper coverage indicated that Baldi had indeed been indicted on the former charge of attempted murder of a policeman, but that this information had not been communicated to Creedmoor, who should not have released him without notifying the district attorney. It was after this inappropriate release that he murdered the teenager. In 1974, Baldi was convicted of this murder and sentenced to 25 years to life. He was also implicated in the stabbing murders of three other women in Queens and someday could stand trial on these charges.

The second case, which also garnered considerable media coverage, was that of Ricardo Caputo, who escaped from Manhattan State Hospital and subsequently allegedly bludgeoned to death a psychologist whom he had met while in Matteawan and whom he had been dating since his transfer to Manhattan State Hospital. According to the *New York Daily News* of October 23, 1974, Caputo was thought to have met Judith Becker in her apartment on Saturday, October 19, after he walked out of the hospital. When her parents called her apartment on Monday and got no answer, the police investigated and found her semi-nude body slumped on her bed with a nylon stocking around her neck. She had been beaten with a blunt instrument. Caputo, a handsome, 25-year-old Argentinian, who was under indictment for the murder three years earlier of his former girl friend, has yet to be captured.

Thus, of the 411 defendants who were released to the community, these were the only two about whom the public heard much. Many of the other 409 were arrested again (44%). Some of them (12%) were involved in crimes against persons. Most, however, committed property crimes, probably associated with their lack of job skills and poor living conditions. When policies for the detention and treatment of incompetent defendants are reviewed, cases like Baldi's and Caputo's are the ones typically cited. What the public and the legislators then often demand are policies that are more restrictive than the experiences of the total group would seem to require. It is important to consider the full range of data to evolve rational social policy.

Rehospitalization

Most studies of criminal recidivism show that numerous prior arrests increase the probability of subsequent arrest. Studies on mental hospitalization also show a strong link between prior and subsequent hospitalizations. Among the incompetent defendants, those previously arrested were the most likely to be rearrested, and those previously hospitalized were the most likely to be rehospitalized. Among these defendants, this association is particularly important, since 82 percent of all the defendants had previously been hospitalized. Thus, it is not surprising that 44 percent of the defendants were rehospitalized during the follow-up period (see table 12). Those defendants with no mental hospitalizations before their incompetency determinations were much less likely to be hospitalized subsequently. Only 22 percent of those with no prior hospitalizations had subsequent hospitalizations. This percentage steadily increased to 32 percent for those with one prior hospitalization, 40 percent for those with two previous hospitalizations, and went up to 57 percent for the defendants who had three or more previous hospitalizations. Thus, as would be expected from their mental hospitalization histories, nearly half of the incompetent defendants returned to mental hospitals after reaching the community.

TABLE 12   Total Subsequent Mental Hospitalizations by Total
Prior Mental Hospitalizations for Incompetent Defendants
Released to the Community

Total subsequent Hospitalizations	Total Prior Hospitalizations							
	0		1		2		3 or more	
	N	%	N	%	N	%	N	%
0	54	78.3	53	67.9	32	60.4	86	43.0
1	7	10.1	10	12.8	10	18.9	34	17.0
2	7	10.1	7	9.0	8	15.1	30	15.0
3 or more	1	1.4	8	10.3	3	5.7	50	25.0
TOTAL	69	99.9	78	100.0	53	100.0	200	100.0

$X^2 = 43.901$; $p < .001$; $C^2 = .314$

With 44 percent of the 411 defendants subsequently arrested and 44 percent rehospitalized, it would be expected that some defendants were both rearrested and rehospitalized. Of the 408 defendants for whom complete information on both arrests and hospitalizations is available, 87 (21%) were both rearrested and rehospitalized. As might be expected, this criminal and hospital recidivism group had more prior arrests and more prior hospitalizations than the group of incompetent defendants as a whole. The multiple recidivism group had an average of four prior arrests and five prior mental hospitalizations. The remainder of the defendant group at risk averaged three prior arrests and three prior hospitalizations. They averaged 32 years of age—close to the average for the entire group. Thus, with prior criminality highly associated with subsequent arrest and prior hospitalizations highly associated with subsequent hospitalization, those defendants who experienced both rearrest and rehospitalization include precisely those who would be expected to be included in either group individually. They would seem to have been multiply handicapped before being found incompetent, and, subsequently, they were multiple recidivists.

Some related questions may be profitably addressed. The first pertains to a basic tenet of all criminal justice diversion programs. Diversion programs have traditionally promised cost savings, rehabilitation, and more humane treatment. Recidivism raises the issue of society's expectation of and right to rehabilitation from the incompetency diversions. This clearly becomes an issue when such a high percentage of these defendants are rearrested and rehospitalized.

Incompetency diversion should not be expected to produce rehabilitation in the usual, criminal justice sense of this term, that is, lower recidivism. When found incompetent, a defendant is shifted out of the criminal justice system and into the mental health system. The justification for this is that the defendant does not possess the mental abilities to participate rationally in a trial. The mental hospitalization is geared toward the defendant's regaining his ability to proceed with a trial. There is nothing in the statutes or mental health treatment goals that suggests that recidivism rates should be the measure of the program's success. While there may be some popular expectations among the public and legislators that psychiatric treatment will make such defendants less dangerous when they return to the community, the legal basis for incompetency diversion does not support these expectations. Incompetency diversion is intended to maintain a balance between the rights of the state and the rights of the individual to due process. Overlooking the fundamental premise of incompetency diversion and judging from the perspective of the general goals of diversion programs leads one to see the recidivism data presented above as central to any conclusions about defendants' "beating a rap." However, we argue to the contrary and interpret our recidivism data as an epilogue that fills out the story about how long and under what conditions these defendants were detained.

Escapees
Defendants who escape from civil mental hospitals have been of particular concern to legislators and the public, and have been

of special interest to us in our considerations of who "beats a rap." As noted in chapter 6, escape and avoidance of prosecution do not always go together. Many defendants are apprehended or return after escapes. Because of the relevance of the escapees, the recidivism of this group was analyzed separately.

Fifty-seven (11%) of the 539 defendants escaped before the final disposition of their criminal charges. In terms of their subsequent arrest and hospitalization, the escapees were quite similar to the other defendants. Of 54 escapees on whom we had information, 26 (48%) were rearrested. This was comparable to the 44 percent for the entire group. Likewise, 9 percent of the escapees were subsequently arrested for violent crimes, compared to 12 percent for the entire group. Of the 56 escapees for whom hospitalization data were available, 25 (45%) were rehospitalized, compared with 44 percent of the total group. Thus, on these major indicators of community adjustment, the escapees caused and encountered trouble at about the same rate as the entire group. The popular conceptions of this group as successfully "beating a rap" and producing a disproportionate amount of future crime is simply inaccurate. The fact that they escape from civil hospitals does not mean that they are an especially dangerous group of incompetent defendants.

This view of the escapees completes the statistical overview of what happened to these 539 incompetent defendants after they returned to the community. Their subsequent criminal activities were similar to those of comparable groups of inmates, and their rehospitalization experiences were comparable to multiple admission mental patients. What might be considered the relatively unsuccessful outcomes among these defendants (44% rearrested and 44% rehospitalized) has little relevance to whether they "beat a rap." This information simply completes a picture and suggests that these defendants continue to behave in the community in a manner that would have been expected had their confinement been in prison rather than in a mental hospital.

We also gathered some information about the living conditions and functioning of these defendants after their release. The next section presents some information about 27 defendants living in New York City after their release.

COMMUNITY INTERVIEWS
The group selected for community follow-up consisted of the first

79 patients known to have returned to the community in New York City. The New York City area was selected because two-thirds of all defendants resided there. We believed that, with this concentration of defendants, our costs of locating them would be manageable. As it turned out, the sheer size and complexity of New York City made location unusually difficult.

The main tools we used for locating the 79 defendants were information gathered in the pretransfer interviews and the hospital records. At the end of the pretransfer interview, we told the defendants that we would be trying to locate some of them after they returned to the community and asked their permission to do so if they were among those chosen for follow-up. If they agreed, we asked for an address where they might be living or where some family member resided who would know where they were living. Also, we scoured the hospital records for addresses of the defendants and of their families before arrest. If they did not wish to be involved, they were removed from the follow-up group. Using this information, two-person teams went knocking on doors searching for defendants who had been back in the community from 4 to 8 weeks.

For various reasons, only 27 of the 79 defendants sought were interviewed, although 55 were located. Of the 79 defendants sought, 10 were reinstitutionalized before they were found, 7 moved out of the New York City area, 1 was deported, 1 joined the military, and 1 died. There were 35 defendants with whom we talked, but 8 refused to be interviewed. Thus, 24 (30%) of those sought could not be located. An example of the kind of detective work required in these locations and some of the frustrations is evident in the case of Douglas Boston. The field notes observed:

10/31/72
    Gregg and I went to ———— Avenue, Brooklyn, a former address of the subject, and were told that he had lived there 2½ years ago. The "super" said Boston had left no forwarding address and did not know of any friends or relatives who might know his whereabouts.
    We also went to the Sloan House Y.M.C.A. on 34th Street, New York City. The man at the desk checked forwarding addresses and could find no one named Douglas Boston. He then checked the files and said that no one by that name was listed as having stayed there, presently or in the past.
    Jerry B. and I checked the Mid-Hudson visitors book and found no visitors.

11/29/72

Gregg and I·visited ——— Street, Brooklyn, the address given
for Douglas Boston in the Brooklyn State Hospital records. The
address belongs to his sister, who hasn't heard from Douglas
since he was hospitalized and who was unaware that he was back in
the community. She suggested that we contact her sister
Mayunice, who is closer to the subject, or another sister Mabel
Boston. We phoned Mabel Boston, who resides at ———
Lafayette Avenue, Brooklyn. She told us that she had not been in
contact with the subject and gave us the phone number of
Mayunice. Mayunice said that the last time she had seen the
subject was in October and that she did not see him on any sort
of regular basis. We gave her the office number and asked her to
contact us if she heard of the whereabouts of her brother.

1/24/73

I phoned the subject's sister, Mayunice Boston, who had said
she might see her brother during the Christmas season. She said
that he had seen her on New Year's Eve and had attempted to
phone us. She gave ——— as her brother's phone number. When
I phoned the subject, he said that he remembered doing an
interview for us when he was at Mid-Hudson, and agreed to see us
some time next week. He said that we should phone him and tell
him when we are coming, after we work out a time that is
convenient to us. The subject is now residing at ——— Jamaica,
New York.

A similar case was that of Joseph Baldi, discussed earlier, who
was one of the 24 cases we were unable to locate. The field notes
report that:

We were not able to reach this follow-up patient by phone, and
when we arrived at his residence, we found that nobody was
home. We tried a little later with the same result. We rang the
doorbells of four neighbors. Nobody answered. On the fifth try,
the lady next door told us she never heard of Mr. Baldi. So we
figured he might be working during the day and, rather than
waiting around for an indefinite period of time, we set out for our
next community contact.

As it turned out, the newspaper details after his murder arrest
noted that he had moved from 143-41 97th Avenue to 88-14 170th
Street, a few blocks away, but no one with whom we talked knew
this.

The 27 defendants interviewed had a wide variety of living
conditions, ranging from a Bowery shelter to comfortable apart-

ments in Forest Hills and single-family homes in Queens. The interviews focused on the defendants' views of the maximum security facilities and on their current living arrangements. Rather than subjects' self-assessments of their functioning, we were satisfied with the global views of the interviewers. These views suggested three very distinct groups among the defendants. One group was almost totally asocial, sleeping most of the day when not watching television, and seen by their family and neighbors as crazy. A second group was more involved in social and work relationships, but had many active delusions or dysfunctional behaviors. The third group was actively involved in social relations, some productive and legal and others marginally productive or illegal, and were apparently able to function independently.

Examples of the asocial group were Miguel Gonzalez and Vincent Tilario. These defendants were described by the interviewers as follows:

Subject's mother answered the door. She spoke only in Spanish but I was able to make her understand that we wanted to speak with her son and that we had seen him when he was at Mid-Hudson. Even though she let us in, she still really didn't understand who we were, and I was unable to explain it to her with my limited knowledge of Spanish. Miguel was sleeping and before she went to wake him up, she indicated that she thought he was "loco." Miguel was quite agitated and hostile when she awakened him and shouted that he "was finished with Mid-Hudson." I walked over to the door so that he could see who I was with the hope that he would remember me from the pretransfer interview. He stated he didn't remember me, but later changed his mind when he came out.

The apartment seemed quite bare, with little to no furniture. Mrs. Gonzalez set up a chair for me opposite Miguel. I interviewed Miguel while Hank and Mrs. Gonzalez stood by. Miguel seemed quite agitated and very annoyed with the interview. Consequently, it was very difficult to follow the interview as planned. We did as much as we could, learning that he did little more than sleep and watch television all day.

Mrs. Tilario is getting very depressed about Vincent. He is not motivated for anything and doesn't do anything but sit home and watch television. She has no life of her own anymore and is afraid to leave Vincent at home alone. Subject has not progressed at all since we last spoke with him. He has been sentenced to five years probation and as a condition of probation is expected to receive psychiatric treatment at the clinic. Mrs. T. says that treatment has been a waste because the Dr. can get no answers from Vincent either.

Mrs. T. says that Vincent does go out on Sundays either bowling with his brother, brother in-law, and father or sometimes to play pool with them. He does this only half-heartedly, though, and will not go out of the house for any other reason except on occasion to go to the store for his mother. He has not looked for work and it is the type of situation which will perpetuate itself unless something is done to force him out. He is accepting his mother's support without any thoughts of ever taking the responsibility to support himself. He is not interested in working or anything and stays glued to the TV all day. He has no friends and no desires to make any.

The level of functioning of these two former defendants and many others like them was much better when they had been interviewed in Mid-Hudson or Matteawan. Under those conditions of treatment and medication, they were much more able to discuss the conditions of maximum security confinement, what they expected to do upon return to the community, and the stigma associated with being labeled criminally insane. We were struck by how they had deteriorated in the community. This deterioration is important because so much of our discussion of incompetency diversion has centered on the dispositional machinations involved and only lightly touched on the fact that some of these defendants were quite disturbed. There was little doubt that some of these men were not competent to stand trial or to function in the community.

An expample of the socially active, but delusional group was Bernacio Ortiz.

Walter [the interviewer] described the subject as a "madman." He talked about being an advisor to the president and the courts. He has authority hang-ups. He showed us all kinds of ID cards and says his name is well thought of in high places. He likes being registered with proper authorities as well.

He was carrying a big knife according to his relatives who were there and who would whisper to Walter that he is crazy and that he can be very frightening. When we left, he shook our hands and embraced us as "amigos."

In sharp contrast were the living situations and social functioning of George Olvetti, who is included in the third group.

2/28/73

George is receiving training as a hairdresser at Bronx State
Hospital (OVR picks up the tab for the training). He does this
four times a week about three hours each day. This is in keeping
with his goal, as he always wanted to be a hairdresser. He likes
working at Bronx State and would much prefer to work in that
environment than in a shop on the outside. There is less pressure
in the hospital. He is also receiveing treatment on an outpatient
basis, taking both medication and group therapy. He finds this
helpful. He feels much better now.

5/25/73

Subject called collect today from school. He was very apologetic
about having missed us. He said that his class was extended till
late and he had to stay. He rushed home and got there at 9:00 P.M.
but we'd already gone. He sounds very happy. He is very excited
about his hairdressing classes. He admits that at first he was very
nervous and was told by his instructor that he was trying too hard.
He has relaxed some and is enjoying it more. He expects to finish
in five months but says that after that he is going to take two more
advanced classes in hair dying and makeup, and this will last for
a while longer. He said his friend with his own hairdressing
shop in the village has invited him to work with him but George
would prefer to work in a more low-keyed area like midtown
Manhattan...

He also stated that he is receiving treatment from a psychiatrist
on the Grand Concourse once per week. This is the same
psychiatrist who worked at Riker's Island and he already knew
George. He feels this doctor is helping him. He takes some
medication to calm his nerves, which helps.

8/27/73

Subject was at home with his brother and the rest of his family
the night we did the interview. He is always excited to see us and
has been one of the most cooperative and, for me, enjoyable
subjects to interview.

George has been doing extremely well since he has gotten out of
Matteawan. He still receives treatment from a private psychiatrist
once a week. He feels this has helped him, as it gives him a chance
to talk things out with someone. He has not been taking the
tranquilizers given him by the doctor, as he prefers to make it
without any form of medication (mostly for fear of dependence).
He said the doctor gave them to him because he believes him to be
high-strung.

Right now, George seems to be involved in a lot of things. He is still attending OVR beautician classes five days a week full time. He works in a beauty shop as part of his training. He seems to like it and will be taking the first in a series of three exams for licensing shortly. In addition, he has just joined the dance company of a Latin Dance Review. He is very excited about it, since he loves to dance. Together, he hardly has time to breath, since he must go to rehearsals every night after school. His only new friends are those in the show and a painter he met whom he doesn't see too often. He is staying away from all of his old friends.

However, a number of those cases in which the persons were functioning well when a first month interview was done showed substantial deterioration by the third or sixth month interview. This type of situation is exemplified by Robert Simpson:

3/1/73
While Jeremy spoke with Robert's grandmother, I attempted to do the subject interview. The subject had, at the first interview, been lucid and cooperative. This time he was also cooperative, in that he seemed to relish the opportunity to talk, however, he was highly delusional. At only one point was I able to get the subject to talk about an actual detail in his life, which was a former job of his. The rest of the time, he told me about his various university degrees and his missions as a bombing pilot for the Viet Cong and the United States Air Force. The subject was able to carry on a very coherent conversation within his delusions and documented his narrative with incidents and places mentioned frequently in press coverage.

8/73
Jerry and I went to subject's home at ——— Jamaica and interviewed Simpson's grandmother. She told us that Robert is rarely at home any more during the day because he goes to Manhattan for some courses he is taking, though she did not know what the courses were or where the school is located. As we were about to drive off in the car, we noticed a man walking in the rain carrying his jacket in his hand and holding what seemed to be an imaginary umbrella in the other hand. The man turned out to be Robert so we went back to the house to talk with him.

Robert is totally disoriented in his present actions. He told us that he is going to NYU and studying dentistry, OBS, working on his Ph.D., etc. He also related that he works during the day at a sandal shop making sandals and jewelry. He complains that everyone in the village is bothering him with their problems and wishes they would leave him alone. He seemed very hyper when we were talking with him and insisted that we have coffee with him.

In reaching any conclusions about the overall level of social functioning of these defendants, some possible biases as a result of the 30 percent nonlocation rate must be noted. Those defendants who had a level of functioning sufficient to use incompetency as a way to "beat a rap" might be those who would least like to be located. Furthermore, with police and mental health records available to us, those defendants who were most capable of independent social functioning might be those who were most mobile and did not again come into contact with police or mental hospitals. So, there is a distinct possibility that the 30 percent not located among the 79 defendants sought were those who were in the best condition. If this is true, the dismal picture our data suggest may not be quite so bleak in reality.

Summing up, we followed a group of individuals who had been arrested an average of three times before their incompetency determinations. Eighty-two percent of them had previously been in mental hospitals. After their return to the community, they functioned as one might expect. They had few job skills, and they lived for the most part in either broken or disturbed families. Their frequency of recidivism and rehospitalization was not surprising. The amount of deterioration of so many defendants between their pretransfer and community interviews was not expected, but helps to explain the recidivism and rehospitalization rates.

The field notes documenting the follow-up make it clear why the 44 percent rearrest rate and the 44 percent rehospitalization rate reported in the previous section of the chapter occurred. These persons, for the most part, are marginal individuals. They return to the same neighborhoods and circumstances associated with many prior arrests and hospitalizations. Their inability to find or keep jobs, their disruptive living situations, and their poor mental adjustment are evident. They are incompetent both socially and as criminals. They get caught over and over again. It is not a very optimistic picture. In all, these defendants did not do well before they were found incompetent and generally they did not appear to be doing well after their return to the community.

Notes

Chapter 1

1. As described by Palmer (1975) this program in Columbus, Ohio, prevented 98 percent of the cases referred from filing criminal complaints. In 97 percent of the cases, the person who originally wanted criminal charges pressed did not file any subsequent charges against the original parties.

2. The generally accepted standards for formally classifying diversion programs are discussed by Watkins (1975). He specifies: (1) intervention in the criminal processing must occur after a criminal act has been committed; (2) the criminal act must be something that has not been decriminalized; and (3) the program must be formalized, serve a definite population and ideally provide preadjudication dispositions.

Chapter 3

1. "Annual Statistical Report 1975 Data Inmate and Parole Populations," table 6. State of New York Department of Correctional Services.

2. In New York, prosecution of a felony cannot occur without a grand jury first handing up an indictment. This requires the district attorney to present evidence to a regularly selected grand jury, which decides whether the strength of the case is sufficient to warrant proceeding to prosecute. If they decide affirmatively,

an indictment is written and prosecution proceeds in the state supreme court. If the grand jury feels the case is too weak, the charges are dismissed.

Chapter 4

1. The coding categories were adapted from N. G. Poythress, "Psychiatric Experts, Guardian Ad Litem Attorneys, and Civil Commitment: Training Lawyers to Cope with Expert Testimony" (Ph.D. dissertation, University of Texas at Austin, May 1977).

Chapter 5

1. All patients' names in this book are pseudonyms, except those taken from newspaper accounts.

2. As part of a community follow-up, described in detail in the Epilogue, 27 defendants were asked about staff brutality. Most of these were in Mid-Hudson during the correctional model phase. The community follow-up provided an opportunity to determine whether the defendants might give a different picture when totally outside the facilities. The patients might report less brutality if they had been overestimating it in order to give us an overly bad picture of their situations, or they might report more brutality because there was no possibility of retribution by the ward staff. Such retribution never occurred after the patient interviews in Mid-Hudson and Matteawan, but could easily have been a concern of the defendants when the pretransfer interviews were done.

Asked if they had seen much brutality while at Mid-Hudson, 18 (69%) of the 26 who answered the question said yes. When asked what types of brutality they had seen, 15 of the 18 described various types of hitting and beating, the other 3 mentioned pushing or shoving of the patients. To determine the frequency with which such alleged brutality occurred, the subjects were asked how often they had seen such behavior by the guards. Of the 17 subjects who said they had seen some and could estimate its frequency, 4 said, "a few times;" 3 said, "about once a week;" 5 said, "twice a week;" and 5 said, "more than two times a week." To further pin down what may have occurred, the subjects were asked if they personally had been the objects of any staff brutality. Seven of the 27 (26%) said yes. Thus, from these responses given under no institutional pressures, it appeared that the amount of staff brutality in the maximum security facilities was realistically assessed by our observations and pretransfer interviews.

Chapter 6

1. New York City is divided into five boroughs—Manhattan, Bronx, Queens, Brooklyn, and Staten Island. These are the legal equivalent of counties in the rest of the state and are sometimes referred to as such. "New York County" is the borough of Manhattan, and "Kings County" is the borough of Brooklyn.

Epilogue

1. Stepwise multiple regression analysis provides additional support for these findings. Prior arrests was the first variable the program entered with a zero-order r equal to .363. Age was the second variable increasing the Multiple R to .391. The third variable was length of time previously in mental hospitals which changed the R to .405. The other three variables included were prior arrest for violent crimes, number of prior hospitalizations and total number of prior convictions. These six variables produced a Multiple R of .406 and an R^2 of .165.

References

Cooke, Gerald; Norman Johnson; and Eric Pogany
   1973 "Factors Affecting Referral to Determine Competency to Stand Trial." *American Journal of Psychiatry* 130:870–75.
Division of Criminal Justice Services, New York State
   1977 New York State Crime and Justice Annual Report. Albany, New York.
Foote, Caleb
   1960 "A Comment on Pre-Trial Commitment of Criminal Defendants." *University of Pennsylvania Law Review* 108:832–46.
Glaser, Daniel
   1969 *The Effectiveness of a Prison and Parole System.* New York: Bobbs-Merrill.
Group for the Advancement of Psychiatry
   1974 Misuse of Psychiatry in the Criminal Courts: Competency to Stand Trial. Vol. 8, rept. 89.
Hess, John H.; Henry B. Pearsall; Donald A. Slichter; and Herbert E. Thomas
   1961 "Incompetency Proceedings." *Michigan Law Review* 59:1078–1100.
Jacoby, Joseph E.
   1975 "Prediction of Dangerousness Among Mentally Ill Of-

fenders." Paper presented for Annual Meeting of the American Society of Criminology, Toronto, Canada.

Laben, Joyce K.; Mark Kashgarian; Donald Nessa; and Lona Davis Spencer
1977 "Reform from the Inside: Mental Health Center Evaluations of Competency to Stand Trial." *Journal of Community Psychology* 5:52–62.

Laczko, Andrew L. et al.
1970 "A Study of Four Hundred and Thirty-Five Court-Referred Cases." *Journal of Forensic Sciences* 15:311–23.

Matthews, Arthur R., Jr.
1970 Mental Disability and the Criminal Law. Chicago: American Bar Association.

McGarry, A. Louis
1972 Competency to Stand Trial and Mental Illness. National Institute of Mental Health. Washington, D.C.: U.S. Government Printing Office.

McGarry, A. Louis and Richard H. Bendt
1969 "Criminal vs. Civil Commitment of Psychotic Offenders: A Seven-Year Follow-Up." *American Journal of Psychiatry* 125:93–100.

Miller, Dorothy and Michael Schwartz
1966 "County Lunacy Commission Hearings: Some Observations of Commitments to a State Mental Hospital." *Social Problems* 14:26–35.

Morris, Norval
1968 "Psychiatry and the Dangerous Criminal." *Southern California Law Review* 41:514–47.

Palmer, John W.
1975 "Pre-Arrest Diversion." *Crime and Deliquency,* 21: 100–108.

Pfeiffer, Eric; Richard Eisenstein; and E. Gerald Bobbs
1967 "Mental Competency Evaluation for the Federal Courts: 1, Methods and Results." *Journal of Nervous and Mental Disease* 144:320–28.

Roesch, Ronald and Stephen L. Golding
1977 A Systems Analysis of Competency to Stand Trial Procedures: Implications for Forensic Services in North Carolina. Urbana, Ill.: National Clearinghouse for Criminal Justice Planning and Architecture.

Rubin, Bernard
1972 "The Prediction of Dangerousness in Mentally Ill Criminals." *Archives of General Psychiatry* 77:397–407.

Scull, Andrew T.
  1977 *Decarceration, Community Treatment and the Deviant—A Radical View.* Englewood Cliffs, N.J.: Prentice-Hall.
Slovenko, Ralph
  1977 "The Developing Law on Competency to Stand Trial." *Journal of Psychiatry and Law.* 5:165-200.
Steadman, Henry J. and Joseph J. Cocozza
  1974 *Careers of the Criminally Insane.* Lexington, Mass.: Lexington Books, D. C. Heath.
  1978 "Selective Reporting and the Public's Misconceptions of the Criminally Insane." *Public Opinion Quarterly* 41 (Winter 1977-78): 523-33.
Steadman, Henry J.; Joseph J. Cocozza; and Sara Lee
  1978 "From Maximum Security to Secure Treatment: Organizational Constraints." *Human Organization.* 37:276-84.
Steadman, Henry J.; Joseph J. Cocozza; and Mary Evans Melick
  1978 "Explaining the Increased Crime Rate of Mental Patients: The Changing Clientele of State Hospitals." *American Journal of Psychiatry* 135:816-20.
Stone, Alan A.
  1975 Mental Health and Law: A System in Transition. Washington, D.C.: U.S. Government Printing Office.
Thornberry, Terence P. and Joseph E. Jacoby
  1976 "The Social Adjustment of the Released Criminally Insane Offender." Paper presented at Annual Meeting of the American Society of Criminology, Tuscon, Arizona.
Tuteur, Werner
  1969 "Incompetency to Stand Trial, A Survey." *Corrective Therapy and Journal of Social Therapy* 15:73-79.
Vann, Carl R.
  1965 "Pre-Trial Decision-Making: An Analysis of the Use of Psychiatric Information in the Administration of Criminal Justice." *University of Detroit Law Journal* 43:13-33.
Vorenberg, Elizabeth and James Vorenberg
  1973 "Early Diversion from the Criminal Justice System: Practice in Search of a Theory." In *Prisoners in America.* Edited by Lloyd E. Ohlin. Englewood Cliffs, N.J.: Prentice-Hall.
Watkins, Ann M.
  1975 Cost Analysis of Correctional Standards: Pretrial Diversion. Vol. 1. National Institute of Law Enforcement and Criminal Justice. Washington: U.S. Government Printing Office.

Wenger, Dennis L. and C. Richard Fletcher
    1969 "The Effect of Legal Counsel on Admissions to a State
        Mental Hospital: A Confrontation of Professions." *Jour-
        nal of Health and Social Behavior* 10:66–72.
Weinstein, Henry C.
    1977 Review of *Competency to Stand Trial and Mental Illness.*
        Journal of Psychiatry and Law. 5:133–38.

Index